Celebrating Twenty Years: Gifts in Honor of the Hood Museum of Art

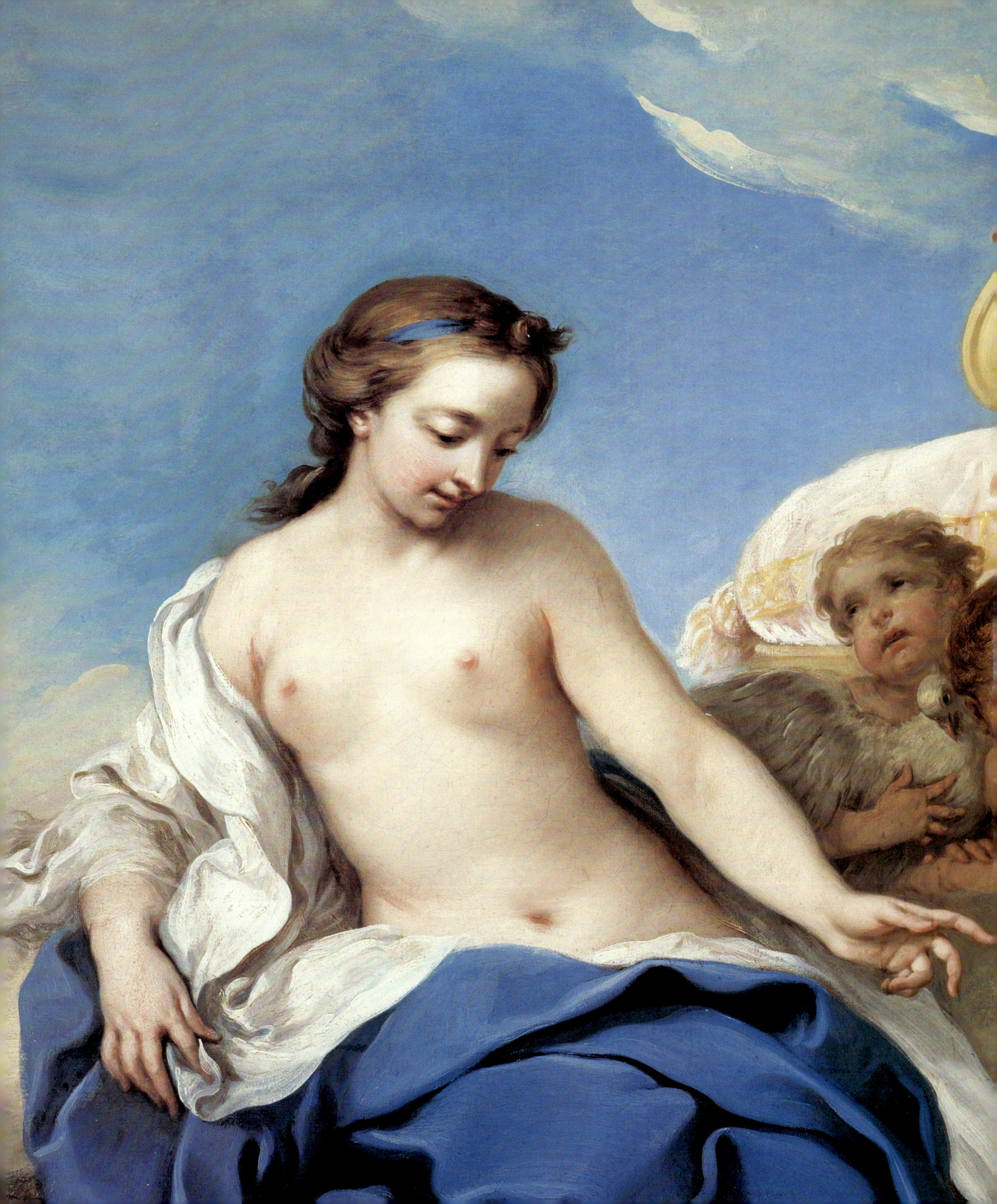

Celebrating Twenty Years

Gifts in Honor of the Hood Museum of Art

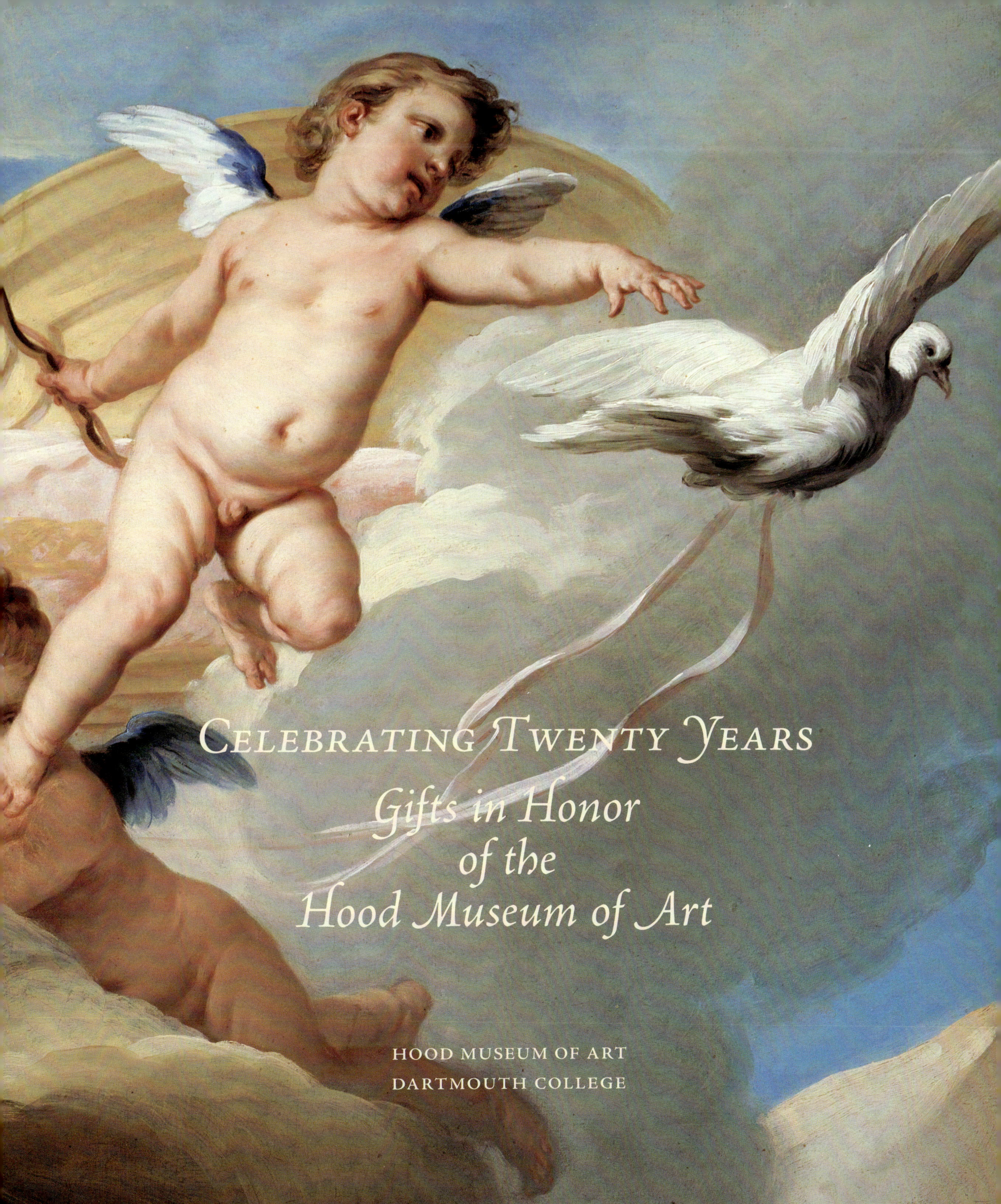

Celebrating Twenty Years

Gifts in Honor of the Hood Museum of Art

Hood Museum of Art
Dartmouth College

Hood Museum of Art, Dartmouth College
Hanover, New Hampshire 03755
www.hoodmuseum.dartmouth.edu

Celebrating Twenty Years: Gifts in Honor of the Hood Museum of Art
Hood Museum of Art, Dartmouth College
Hanover, New Hampshire
June 11–December 11, 2005

This exhibition was generously funded by gifts to the Hood Museum of Art.

Edited by Nils Nadeau
Designed by Glenn Suokko
Printed by Capital Offset Company Inc.
Photography by
Susan Byrne: cat. no. 19
Jacques Cressaty: cat. no. 34 (a and b)
Addison Doty: cat. no. 39
Paul Foster: cat. no. 8
Serge Hambourg: p. 15
Jeffrey Nintzel: cat. nos. 2 (a–m), 3, 4, 5, 10, 11, 12 (a and b), 14, 15, 16, 17, 18, 21, 22, 23 (comparative image), 24, 25 (a and b), 26, 27, 28, 29, 30, 32, 33, 35, 38, 40f
George Roos: cat. no. 42
Bruce M. White: cat. nos. 6, 9

Cover: J. Alden Weir, *Chrysanthemums*, 1888, oil on canvas (detail). Promised gift of Jonathan L. Cohen, Class of 1960, Tuck 1961

Frontispiece: Carle Vanloo, *Venus Requesting Vulcan to Make Arms for Aeneas*, about 1735, oil on canvas (detail). Purchased through a gift from Jane and W. David Dance, Class of 1940, and the Mrs. Harvey P. Hood W'18 Fund

Library of Congress Cataloging-in-Publication Data

Hood Museum of Art.
Celebrating twenty years : gifts in honor of the Hood Museum of Art / [Katherine W. Hart ... et al.].
p. cm.
Catalog of an exhibition held June 11–Dec. 11, 2005.
Includes bibliographical references.
ISBN 0-944722-29-6 (pbk.)
1. Hood Museum of Art—Exhibitions. 2. Art—Private collections—United States—Exhibitions. 3. Art—New Hampshire—Hanover—Exhibitions. I. Hart, Katherine W. II. Title.
N575.A6 2005
708.142'3—dc22

2005009341

ISBN 0-944722-29-6 (pbk.)

Contents

Donors to the Exhibition

AXA Art Insurance Ltd., UK
Jane and Raphael Bernstein
Richard J. Blum, Class of 1953
Lois and H. W. Broido Jr., Class of 1951, Tuck 1952
Jeffrey R. Brown, Class of 1961
Frieda and Prentiss Carnell, Class of 1956
Jonathan L. Cohen, Class of 1960, Tuck 1961
Ellen and Theodore Conant
William P. Curry, Class of 1957
Jane and W. David Dance, Class of 1940
Robert Dance, Class of 1977
Franklin Davidson M.D., Class of 1955
Monroe Denton, Class of 1968
Kira Fournier and Benjamin Schore Fund for Contemporary Sculpture
Valerie Franklin
Hugh J. Freund, Class of 1967
Sondra Gilman and Celso M. Gonzalez-Falla
Jamie and Haim Handwerker
Dr. Michel Hersen and Victoria Jenkins Hersen
Patricia Hewitt and Dale C. Christensen Jr., Class of 1969
Charles Hood, Class of 1951
Mrs. Harvey P. Hood W'18 Fund
Mr. and Mrs. Jack Huber, Class of 1963
Jim Hunt and Maggie Fellner Hunt, Class of 1978
Emily Henderson Graves Jones
Fannie and Alan Leslie M.D., Class of 1930, Medical School 1931
Andrew E. Lewin, Class of 1981
Harry T. Lewis Jr., Class of 1955, Tuck 1956, DP
Madeleine and Stephen Lister, Class of 1963
Micaela and Jack Mendelsohn, Class of 1956
Thomas F. O'Neil III Trust
Bart Osman, Class of 1990, Tuck 1996
Harley and Stephen C. Osman, Class of 1956, Tuck 1957
Scott Osman, Class of 1980
Eric Richards
George T. M. Shackelford, Class of 1977
Dr. David G. Stahl, Class of 1947
Frank P. Stetz
Catherine Dail Weil, Class of 1985

Foreword

Over the twenty years since the Hood Museum of Art opened its doors, it has built upon its strengths to become a much-admired cultural institution—one that reflects Dartmouth's high standards of excellence and intellectual achievement. In the museum's first accreditation report by the American Association of Museums in 1989, the evaluators wrote that the College's museum had become "a national model beyond its splendid facilities, successful for the nature of its relationship to the whole campus and its internal organization." The reaccreditation reviewers in 2000 added, "In the intervening ten years, the Hood has refined its operation on every level, and become as fine a museum as one can find in this country. Perhaps the biggest changes in the Hood, however, pertain to its broader and more inclusive interpretation of its mission, particularly as regards education, the cultural and intellectual resonances of its art, and the diversity of its audiences."

The success of the Hood Museum of Art is due in great part to the excellent leadership of Dartmouth's provosts. Agnar Pytte (1982–85) played a key role, overseeing the design of the magnificent new building by Charles Moore and Centerbrook Architects, as well as the museum's construction. He was ably followed by John Strobehn (1987–93), P. Bruce Pipes (1993–94), Lee C. Bollinger (1994–97), Constance Brinckerhoff (1998–99), and Susan Westerberg Prager (1999–2001). Barry Scherr, who became provost in 2001, offers continued leadership as an invaluable advisor. I remember my own service as provost from 1997 to 1998 as an experience that even further increased my admiration for the museum.

The foresight and vision of the Hood's directors during the period since its founding cannot be overestimated. Each left the museum a stronger place. Dartmouth will be forever grateful to Jacqueline Baas (1985–88), former director of the Berkeley Art Museum and now an independent scholar and curator; James Cuno (1989–91), now director of the Art Institute of Chicago; Timothy Rub (1991–99), now director of the Cincinnati Art Museum; and most recently Derrick Cartwright (2000–2004), currently director of the San Diego Museum of Art. Today, we are looking forward to the arrival of Brian Kennedy, former director of the National Gallery of Australia, who will assume leadership of the museum in July 2005.

In recognition of the museum's accomplishments over the last two decades, generous alumni, alumnae, and friends of Dartmouth have promised or made over forty gifts to its collections. We honor these contributions to the museum's future in both the exhibition and the catalogue for *Celebrating Twenty Years: Gifts in Honor of the Hood Museum of Art.* I offer Dartmouth's deep thanks to this dedicated group of donors and to the many other friends and colleagues who have also helped make the Hood Museum of Art an extraordinary place of learning and discovery for our students—and for all of us.

James Wright
President, Dartmouth College

Preface and Acknowledgments

A museum's collections comprise its greatest asset. A distinguished art or anthropology collection takes many years to develop, not only because museum-quality objects are rare but also because their value makes it very expensive for an institution to acquire them. It would be almost impossible today to start a strong museum without a pre-existing collection upon which to build. Dartmouth College has been fortunate to have had over 230 years to develop the collections that now reside in the Hood Museum of Art. The history of the collections began with the donation of a mastodon tooth in 1772, just three years after the college's founding, and they have grown since that time to over 65,000 objects. Most of these items have come to Dartmouth as gifts from generous alumni and friends, often in honor or memory of fellow graduates. In the last twenty years, a significant number of works have also been added to the collection through endowment funds. These important resources help the museum's curators shape the collection in ways that will benefit students, faculty, and the general public by filling gaps and building upon strengths.

To celebrate the twentieth anniversary since the building of the Hood and the joining of the art and anthropology collections under one roof, the curators decided to ask the museum's supporters among alumni and friends to donate works of art, or to promise future donations of specific works, in honor of the occasion. The wonderful evidence of their generosity, a rich cornucopia representing a wide range of cultures and media, has been gathered together in this catalogue and its accompanying exhibition. We are extremely gratified that so many works of art have been given and lent at this time, and I extend my sincere and heartfelt gratitude to the donors: AXA Art Insurance Ltd., UK; Jane and Raphael Bernstein; Richard J. Blum, Class of 1953; Lois and H. W. Broido Jr., Class of 1951, Tuck 1952; Jeffrey R. Brown, Class of 1961; Frieda and Prentiss Carnell, Class of 1956; Jonathan L. Cohen, Class of 1960, Tuck 1961; Ellen and Theodore Conant; William P. Curry, Class of 1957; Jane and W. David Dance, Class of 1940; Robert Dance, Class of 1977; Franklin Davidson M.D., Class of 1955; Monroe Denton, Class of 1968; the Kira Fournier and Benjamin Schore Fund for Contemporary Sculpture; Valerie Franklin; Hugh J. Freund, Class of 1967; Sondra Gilman and Celso M. Gonzalez-Falla; Jamie and Haim Handwerker; Dr. Michel Hersen and Victoria Jenkins Hersen; Patricia Hewitt and Dale C. Christensen Jr., Class of 1969; Charles Hood, Class of 1951; Mr. and Mrs. Jack Huber, Class of 1963; Maggie Hunt, Class of 1978; Emily Henderson Graves Jones; Fannie and Alan Leslie M.D., Class of 1930, Medical School 1931; Andrew E. Lewin, Class of 1981; Harry T. Lewis Jr., Class of 1955, Tuck 1956, DP; Madeleine and Stephen Lister, Class of 1963; Micaela and Jack Mendelsohn, Class of 1956; the Thomas F. O'Neil III Trust; Bart Osman, Class of 1990, Tuck 1996; Harley and Stephen C. Osman, Class of 1956, Tuck 1957; Scott Osman, Class of 1980; Eric Richards; George T. M. Shackelford, Class of 1977; Dr. David G. Stahl, Class of 1947; Frank P. Stetz; and Catherine Dail Weil, Class of 1985. Monroe Denton, Class of 1968, played a crucial role in the donation of *Arch* by Richard Artschwager, and we owe him a debt of gratitude as well.

I also would like to acknowledge the important role played in the realization of the exhibition and catalogue by former director Derrick Cartwright and by the curators of the museum: Barbara MacAdam, Jonathan L. Cohen Curator of American Art; T. Barton Thurber, Curator of European Art; Barbara Thompson, Curator of African, Oceanic, and Native American Collections; Katherine Hart, Interim Director and Barbara C. and

Harvey P. Hood 1918 Curator of Academic Programming; and Margaret Lind, Assistant Curator (and Class of 2002). The four curators and assistant curator were joined by a special project intern, Victoria Corder, Class of 2005, in writing the excellent catalogue entries on the objects in the exhibition. In addition, Margaret Lind arranged for photography and also wrote the majority of the exhibition labels. Other important contributors on the Hood staff to the catalogue and exhibition's success are Juliette Bianco, Kellen Haak, Nils Nadeau, Nancy McLain, Kathleen O'Malley, Cynthia Gilliland, Deborah Haynes, Theresa Delemarre, Roberta Shin, Patrick Dunfey, Sharon Reed, Mary Ann Hankel, Kris Bergquist, John Reynolds, and Matt Zayatz. Jeffrey Nintzel, who has provided the museum with his photography services for the last twenty years, did much of the photography for the catalogue, and Glenn Suokko created its elegant design. The Williamstown Conservation Lab was instrumental in cleaning several works in preparation for the exhibition. Barbara MacAdam would also like to extend special thanks to Hank Taron of Tradewind Antiques, who provided his expert knowledge on the history of canes and on Charles Hood's cane collection in particular. The curators would like to thank Carolyn Pelzel, Elizabeth Spencer, Ann Root Keith, Linda Plumb, Nancy Felix, and Brenda Hillyer in the Development Office of the College for their unstinting efforts on the museum's behalf. I would also like to extend my thanks to Mary Gorman, Executive Officer to the Provost. During the interim period between directors, she has served as a liaison to the Board of Overseers and participated in the oversight of the museum on behalf of the provost's office.

It has been my privilege as provost of Dartmouth College to act as administrative overseer of the Hood Museum of Art during the last four years. I would like to thank Derrick Cartwright for his leadership as director of the museum during this period. I would also like to thank the members of the Board of Overseers of the Hopkins Center and Hood Museum of Art, whose dedication to the museum's wellbeing has been an important factor in its success as a national model for academic museums. At the end of this catalogue, we have listed the major donors to the museum's spaces and the individuals who have been instrumental in the development of the collections over the twenty years of the Hood's existence: generous alumni and friends who have established acquisition endowments, donors of works of art and artifacts, donors of current use funds for acquisitions, and the Lathrop Fellows of the Hood Museum of Art, whose membership dues are directly used for acquisitions. To these donors and to those who have contributed to this exhibition we owe our deepest gratitude. We look forward to the next twenty years of the museum. The wonderful support of these donors is an excellent sign that there will be as much for our successors to celebrate in 2025 as there is today.

Barry Scherr
Provost, Dartmouth College

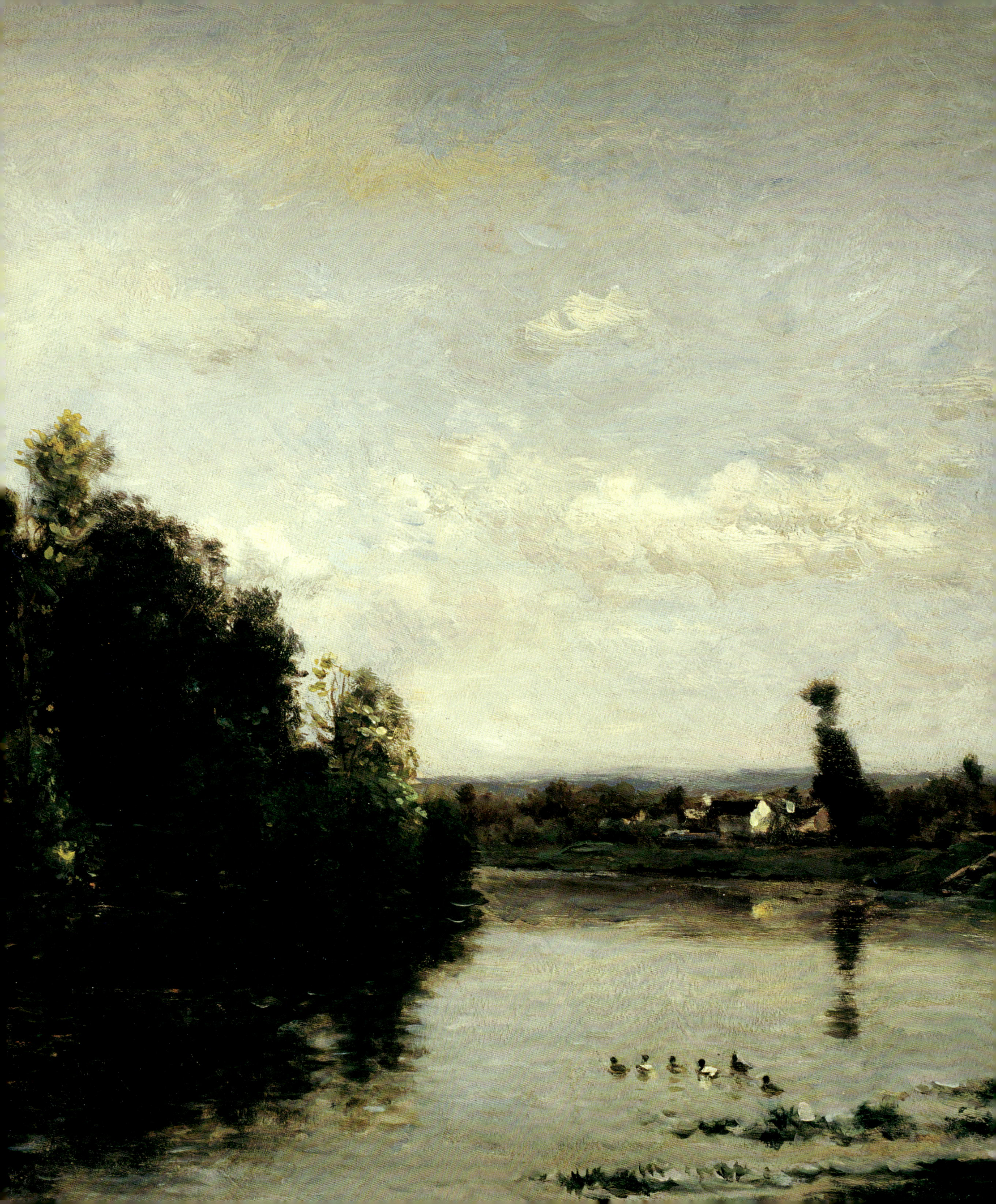

Introduction

> Wandering through clear chambers where the general effect made preferences almost as impossible as if they had been shocks, pausing at open doors where vistas were long and bland, she would, even if she had not already known, have discovered for herself that Poynton was the record of a life. It was written in great syllables of colour and form, the tongues of other countries and the hands of rare artists. It was all France and Italy, with their ages composed to rest. . . . To give it all up, to die to it—that thought ached in her breast. . . . [T]he advent of the others could only be, by the same law, a great vague menace, the ruffling of a still water.
>
> —Henry James, *The Spoils of Poynton*, 1896

In his novella *The Spoils of Poynton* Henry James chronicles the role that highly prized possessions play within the lives of his characters. The "spoils" of the title are Poynton House objects so important to Mrs. Gareth, their owner and collector, that she judges her future daughter-in-law to be incapable of appreciating them and therefore a woman not worthy of her son. Her defiant refusal to relinquish the possessions of the family estate upon the pending marriage of her son is the act around which the narrative revolves. At the center of this story, Poynton's beautiful furnishings and art are a presence equal to that of any character in the book, and separation from them is an imagined sorrow equivalent to death.

Collecting, as represented in James's novel, is an expression of desire. What we possess becomes a part of who we are—an expression of the self and of that with which we want to be associated. The desire to possess an object can excite powerful unconscious desires or memories of past events or feelings. The buyer of a work of art, or even a simple tourist's souvenir, may expect that the object's essence—perhaps the aura of its beauty, the associative values of its history, the spiritual nature of its subject, or the exoticism of its origins—will transfer to its owner. Or perhaps it will serve as a reminder of the best and worst of human existence—the beauty of a flower seen in the soft light of dawn, or a clever comment upon human folly or weakness. The collector of contemporary art may feel that the excitement of the work's immediacy and its connection to the present, its embodiment of current cultural synergies or transgressions, will present its owners as equally vital and engaged.

The curators of the Hood Museum of Art—Barbara MacAdam, Bart Thurber, Barbara Thompson, and myself—understand this close bond between collector and object. When we each ventured to ask alumni and friends to consider parting with one or more of their own artistic treasures, we always

Opposite: Charles-François Daubigny, *The Banks of the Oise River at Mériel*, 1867, oil on panel (detail). Promised gift of Patricia Hewitt and Dale C. Christensen Jr., Class of 1969

kept this relationship in mind. The gifts and promised gifts chronicled in this catalogue, therefore, speak of the deep feeling among this group of donors for the museum and the college it serves. *Celebrating Twenty Years: Gifts in Honor of the Hood Museum of Art*, which marks the twentieth anniversary of the splendid Charles Moore and Centerbrook Architects museum building on the Dartmouth campus, without question documents a remarkable moment in the history of the museum's collecting. It is with great humility that we accept these works of art into the museum's collection—their inclusion in this exhibition is cause for great celebration all on its own.

As individuals who have devoted our professional lives to the care and interpretation of objects, the Hood's curators know from experience the lasting impact that these works of art will have on the students, faculty, and visitors who will see them in the next six months of their display, and who will also have the chance to enjoy and study them at the museum in the future. The history of these works as part of their collectors' lives will be recorded and documented, and each of them will be seen in many different contexts as part of an academic museum's collection. When displayed in association with other selected objects in the Hood's collections or shown in classes on varying subjects, the objects in this catalogue will continue to be interpreted in different contexts and be valued for different reasons. Matthew Pillsbury's *George Spencer, Seducing the Babysitter*, for instance, is a photograph that has already been seen in a film and television studies course on the spaces of television, and it will soon be shown in a studio art course on photography. Other photographs that will enrich the collection are a rare salt paper print by Félix Teynard of an Egyptian archaeological site, a Lewis Hine image of a child worker, a major color photograph, *Piss Elegance*, from Andres Serrano's historically important series that included the famous work *Piss Christ*, a stunning color print of shipbreaking in Bangladesh by Edward Burtynsky, six black-and-white prints from a larger series by Robert Stivers, and a large color image of the quickly changing urban landscape in China by Sze Tsung Leong. George Bellows's magnificent lithograph *Village Massacre*, part of a group of World War I prints that helped prompt the United States to enter the war in 1917, will join two other powerful lithographs by the artist from the same series. Similarly, Paul Sample's painting *Speech Near Brewery* will be reunited with the oil sketch that is currently in the Hood's collection and become part of the museum's larger repository of Paul Sample's works. *Village Massacre* will also be seen, along with James Nachtwey's photograph of a wounded child in El Salvador, as part of a related body of work in the collection that deals with the subject of the impact of war on civilian populations, including etchings in Goya's eight-print series *Disasters of War*.

The museum does have a small collection of decorative arts, but nothing as comprehensive as the promised gift of a marvelous collection of American and European canes, beautifully made in a rich panoply of media. In this area, as well, the museum will receive two richly glazed works by the late ceramicist Beatrice Wood, a jar by the Native American artists Maria and Julian Martinez, who are famous for the lustrous black surface of their pots, and arguably the most important tile created by the Boston arts and crafts pottery firm of Grueby Faience Company. The two Australian paintings by Magdalena Ungwanaka and Pansy Martin Napangardi and the Haitian painted objects by André Pierre, Sisson Blanchard, and another unknown Vodou artist are the first works of this type to come to the Hood, further enriching a wide and diverse collection of non-Western art. The gift of a Yoruba religious sculpture from Nigeria is also an important contribution to the museum's African holdings.

Other welcome additions include important works by Charles-François Daubigny, William Trost Richards, Jesse Talbot, John Adams Parker, J. Alden Weir, Irving Wiles, John Folinsbee, Alexander Archipenko, Rufino Tamayo, Jennifer Bartlett, and Richard Artschwager, as well as a delightful oil sketch by Dennis Miller Bunker and a lovely landscape pastel by Robert Henri. The Weir *Chrysanthemums* will serve as a much-needed addition to the museum's American collection, which has few nineteenth-century still lifes. Frank Stetz has given the museum a large collection of paintings by the mid-nineteenth-century American painter James Cafferty—represented here by the delightful painting *Preparing to Fish*—that were collected by the late David Stewart Hull, a member of Dartmouth's Class of 1960 and the leading authority on Cafferty's work. In addition, the wonderfully descriptive nineteenth-century watercolor by Eugène Ciceri of a work site outside Paris will contribute to the museum's other holdings that show French life of the period. We are also delighted to have been promised what will be the museum's first prints by the eccentric visionary James Ensor and a color woodcut by the master printmaker Gustave Baumann.

In the area of post-1945 art, the works by Vito Acconci and Carolee Schneemann will be our first examples of original documentations of performance works, and woodcuts by Sandy Walker, a monumental paper pulp piece by Chuck Close, and a complex eighteen-plate lithograph by Terry Winters will join a growing collection of master prints in the museum's works on paper collection. Contemporary works by Kathleen Gilje and Paul Chan will enrich the collection through their engagement with issues such as the relationship between copy and original and the meaning of monuments in a post–September 11 world, respectively. Lastly, the magnificent canvas by Carle Vanloo is the first large-scale, multifigure European mythological painting to enter the collection, filling a long-recognized gap.

It is the continual reexamination of the object that makes a museum a living repository of what we and our predecessors have collected, of what we and they value, and of what will represent our purchasers and donors in perpetuity. In his contribution to his recent book of essays by museum directors, *Whose Muse? Art Museums and the Public Trust*, James Cuno, former director of the Hood Museum of Art and now director of the Art Institute of Chicago, states: "The museum as historian—and most of us who work in museums were trained as historians—wants to connect the dots, to make sense of the things it has as a collection and not as an accumulation of discrete things. The critic or connoisseur attends the individual object; the historian seeks to explain a pattern of relationships between objects. At best, the museum wants to do both, simultaneously." When a work of art enters an academic museum collection, it not only becomes the legacy of who has owned it in the past, it also becomes part of the large repository of a public institution of higher learning. Museum professionals as well as students and faculty will connect the dots, examining a given work within a variety of contexts, including those formed by other works in the museum.

As Cuno infers, the Hood Museum of Art's collections, like many other museum collections, are varied and idiosyncratic, and some of their greatest riches stem from the imaginations and collecting impulses of individual curators and donors. In some instances the curator has been a director, such as Jan van der Marck, who in the mid-1970s was responsible for purchasing a great many then-contemporary works, including Sol LeWitt's minimalist sculpture *Incomplete Open Cube 8-14*. Van der Marck also attracted the gifts in honor of George Macunias that comprise our large holding of Fluxus objects. (Fluxus is the sobriquet of a late-1950s and early-1960s international group of avant-garde artists dedicated to ephemeral and performance-oriented art.) Jacqueline Baas, director from 1985 until 1988, acquired the outstanding collection of over three hundred drawings by José Clemente Orozco. Cuno, director from 1989 through 1991, commissioned the large Joel Shapiro sculpture for the Bedford Courtyard; Timothy Rub, director of the museum from 1991 through 1999, purchased, among other works, a major sculpture by Ursula von Rydingsvard as well as a large abstract expressionist canvas by Robert Motherwell; and Derrick Cartwright added to the collection major drawings by Agnes Martin and Eva Hesse and a figural sculpture by Juan Muñoz.

Unexpected treasures have come from collectors such as James Meeker, Class of 1958, who gave the historically significant pop art painting *Standard Station, Amarillo, Texas* by Ed Ruscha, and William Rubin, the former chief curator of the Museum of Modern Art, who gave the museum its major painting by Mark Rothko, *Orange and Lilac over Ivory*. Raphael and Jane Bernstein have given a wonderful selection of works by Romare Bearden. Frank L. Harrington, Class of 1924, donated an outstanding collection of early silver made in Massachusetts, and Frank C. and Clara B. Churchill and Guido R. Rahr Sr. gave rich collections of Native American art and artifacts. The Franklin family chose the Hood Museum of Art to be the beneficiary of a large collection of Melanesian art that was amassed by Harry Franklin, marking this as one of the most important and largest repositories of work from this region in the country. Another important gift received by the museum was a large group of Old Master prints by Mantegna, Dürer, Rembrandt, Callot, Goya, and others, from Jean and Adolph Weil, Class of 1935. One of Mr. Weil's favorite artists was Rembrandt, whose work he came to know through his mother's interest in the artist's paintings. During his lifetime, Weil assembled a superb collection of lifetime impressions of Rembandt's work, and upon his death his wife, Jean, gave twenty-nine of his etchings, as well as a great many superb Old Master prints, to the museum in honor of her husband. His greatest joy was that these incredible works would inspire countless students at the time of their gift and in perpetuity—students who would be able to study them in class in the museum's Bernstein Study Storage Center, in close proximity and without a barrier between them and their surfaces.

All of these works and many others given by generous donors make this collection what it is and help shape what it will be in the future. To the people whose names are listed at the front of this catalogue, we at the Hood Museum of Art give our heartfelt thanks. They and the others who are listed at the back of this catalogue have made a leap of faith and entrusted their works not just to a public museum but to an institution of higher learning that seeks to engage and startle students into experiences that awaken the mind and the passions. You have given over a part of yourselves, and no one knows this better than we who strive to make museums integral to the lives of those who enter them.

KATHERINE W. HART
Interim Director
Barbara C. and Harvey P. Hood 1918 Curator of Academic Programming

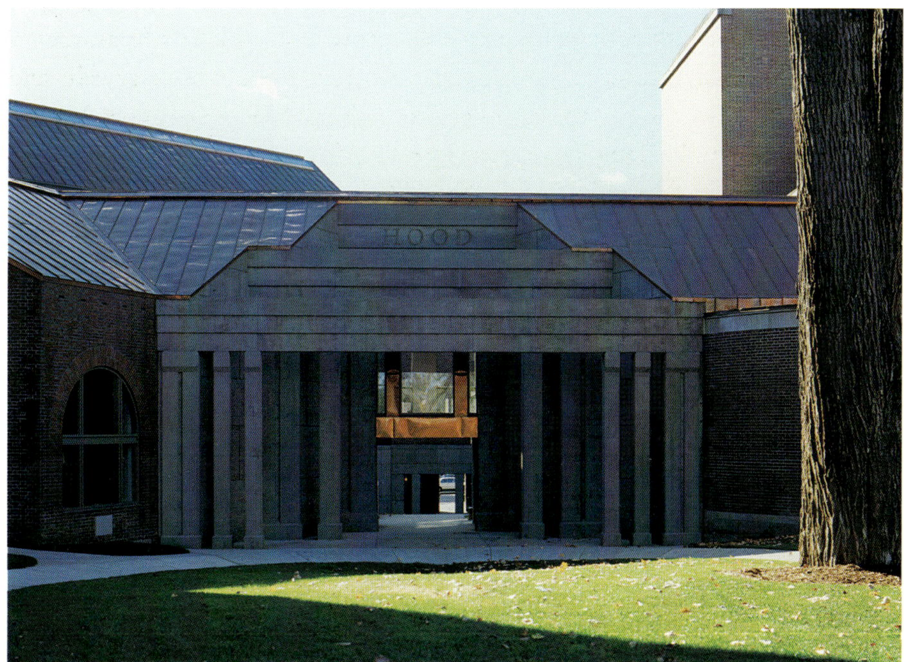

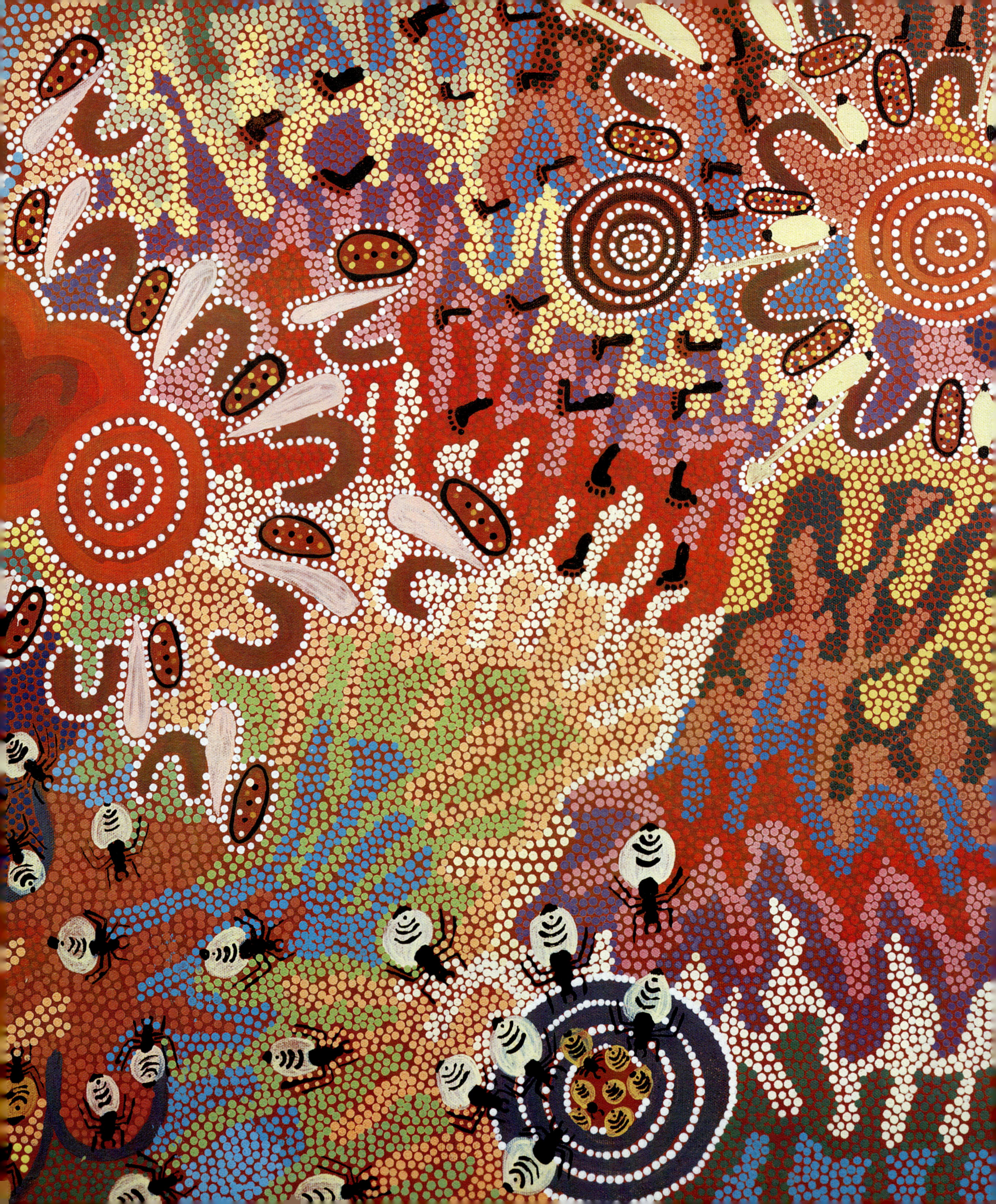

Catalogue

Victoria V. Corder, Class of 2005 [**VVC**]: Special Project Intern

Katherine W. Hart [**KWH**]: Interim Director and Barbara C. and Harvey P. Hood 1918 Curator of Academic Programming

Margaret W. Lind, Class of 2002 [**MWL**]: Assistant Curator

Barbara J. MacAdam [**BJM**]: Jonathan L. Cohen Curator of American Art

Barbara Thompson [**BT**]: Curator of African, Oceanic, and Native American Collections

T. Barton Thurber [**TBT**]: Curator of European Art

All dimensions are given in inches. For objects where one descriptive dimension is sufficient, "L" refers to length, "H" refers to height, and "Diam" refers to diameter. Otherwise, height precedes width precedes depth. For printed works, the dimensions refer to the plate size.

Opposite: Magdalena Ungwanaka, *Honey Ant Dreaming*, 1987, acrylic on canvas (detail). Promised gift of Fannie and Alan Leslie M.D., Class of 1930, Medical School 1931

1 **CHARLES-ANDRÉ VANLOO**

called Carle Vanloo, French, 1705–1765

Venus Requesting Vulcan to Make Arms for Aeneas

About 1735
Oil on canvas
50¾ x 38¾ in.

Purchased through a gift from Jane and W. David Dance, Class of 1940, and the Mrs. Harvey P. Hood W'18 Fund

In this work Venus, the goddess of love, wrapped in bright blue and white drapery, looks at and gestures toward Vulcan, the god of fire. According to a scene from the eighth book of Virgil's *Aeneid*, the female deity asked her consort to forge armor and weapons for her half-mortal son, Aeneas, a Trojan prince. While the Cyclopes labor in the lower left corner, Vulcan seems to yearn for her approval of the completed items. According to the same legend, Aeneas's eventual triumph led to the founding of a Trojan settlement in Rome, from whom later inhabitants descended. The subject appears in numerous European paintings from the sixteenth through the mid-eighteenth centuries.

Carle Vanloo completed this picture soon after he had arrived in Paris from a six-year sojourn in Italy, where he received prestigious awards and worked for prominent patrons in Rome and Turin. By 1737 the artist would establish himself as a professor at the French Royal Academy and receive the first of a number of high-ranking appointments. During the short time between his return and the commencement of his extraordinarily successful career as one of the leading painters in eighteenth-century France, Vanloo executed several works that demonstrated his ability to assimilate various stylistic influences. In many cases he combined classical figural types and a fashionable rococo palette to create mythological subjects, which were acclaimed for their refined design and command of diverse artistic traditions. *Venus Requesting Vulcan to Make Arms for Aeneas* revealed Vanloo's mastery of both antiquity and anatomy, and it contributed to his reputation for producing imaginative compositions based on the tenets of the so-called Grand Style that were aimed at introducing a new grandeur and nobility in French painting. From this point onward, Vanloo never lacked official commissions, and his works were highly regarded at future Salons.

TBT

Bailey, Colin B. *The Loves of the Gods: Mythological Painting from Watteau to David.* New York: Rizzoli, in conjunction with Kimbell Art Museum, 1992. See esp. 384 and 387n19.

Dandré-Bardon, Michel François. *Vie de Carle Vanloo.* Paris: Chez Desaint, 1765.

Réau, Louis. "Carle Vanloo, 1705–1765." *Archives de l'Art Français.* Paris: Nogent-le-Rotrove, 1938: p. 65, no. 105.

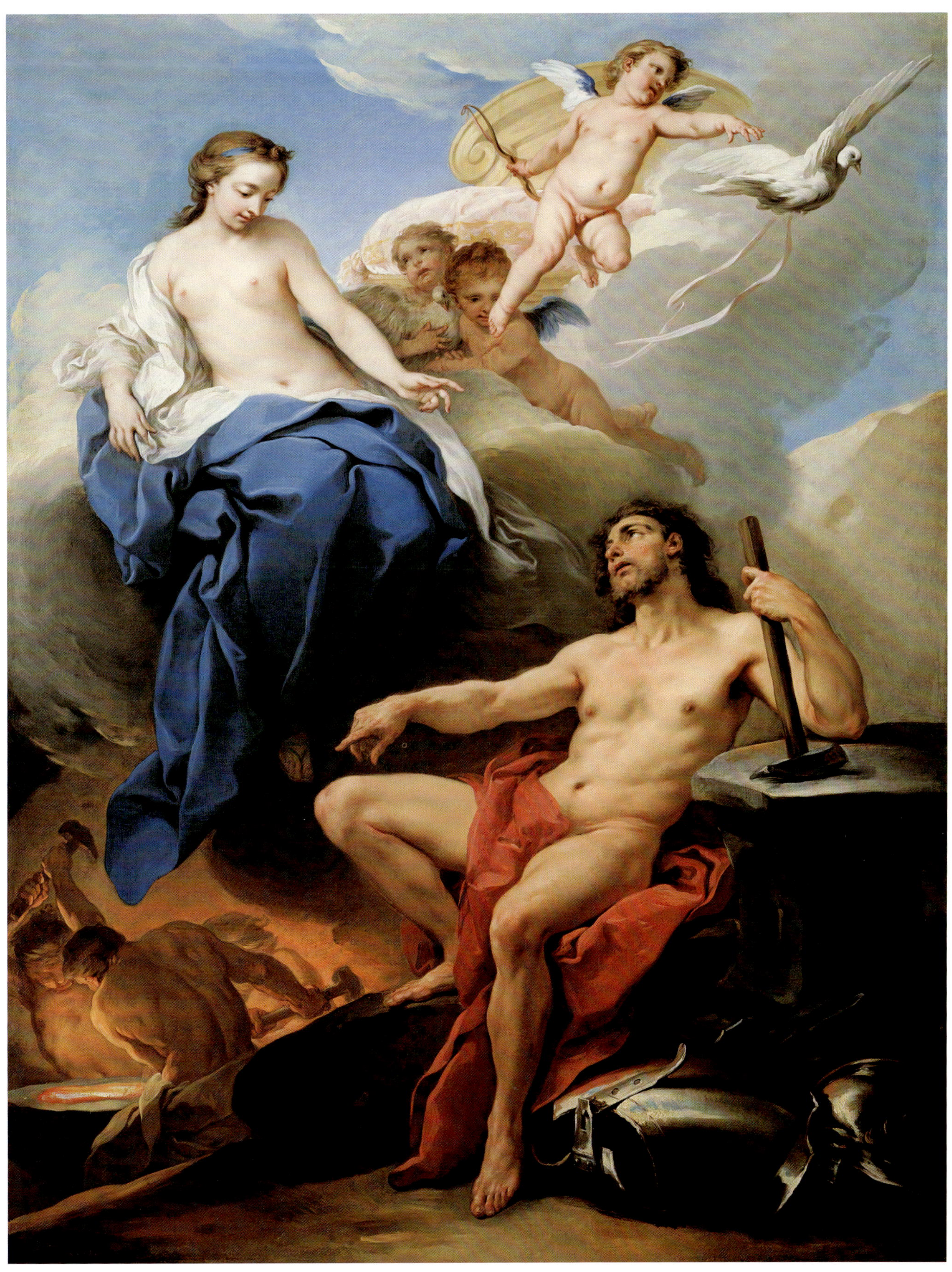

2 Canes

Promised gifts of Charles Hood,
Class of 1951

a) English, unidentified maker
Piqué pomander cane
Dated 1711
Elephant ivory handle, silver collar, malacca shaft, brass and iron ferrule
L: 36½ in.
Inscribed on collar: John Shaw, 1711

b) American, unidentified maker
Phrenology head cane
ca. 1850
Elephant ivory handle, hardwood shaft, white metal and iron ferrule
L: 34 in.

c) American, unidentified maker
Cane with bird handle
ca. 1850
Whale ivory handle, baleen shaft and ferrule
L: 35¾ in.

d) Probably American, unidentified maker
Architectural nautical cane
ca. 1850
Whale ivory "Turk's-head knot" handle and whalebone shaft with open twisted columns
L: 34½ in.

e) American, unidentified maker
Cane with "lady's leg" handle
ca. 1860
Walrus ivory handle, narwhal shaft, exotic wood collar inlaid with ivory
L: 34 in.

Canes, or walking sticks, as they are also termed, have been made and used around the globe since ancient times. Their function has depended largely on their historic and social settings. In some contexts they have served as purely symbolic or ritualistic objects, and in others as primarily a practical means of physical support. Over the past few hundred years in Western societies they have functioned as elegant fashion accessories for both sexes, as important markers of social status, and at times as personal weapons. Canes have also recorded historic events, marked ceremonial occasions, and proclaimed their owner's political allegiances. In their production and artistry, canes vary tremendously in materials and techniques as well as iconography and style. While many have been made with precious materials by highly trained artisans employed by workshops or large firms (such as Tiffany and Company), others, often referred to as "folk canes," are made by single individuals, usually self-taught, who independently handcraft readily accessible materials. Additionally, some canes were fashioned to contain a myriad of hidden utilitarian objects. These are referred to as "gadget" or "system" canes (such as the piqué pomander cane [a]).

This small selection from a large, outstanding cane collection can only hint at the extraordinary variety of approaches taken over the years toward the production and use of canes. The earliest example in this group is an English piqué cane dating to 1711 (a). This type of walking stick is characterized by a simple elephant tusk ivory handle ornamented with delicate linear patterns of inset silver studs. In this cane, the top of the ivory handle unscrews to reveal a small compartment for storing a piece of fabric saturated with healing herbs or salts as protection against illness. Holes in the cap allow one to smell the aroma.

Imported elephant tusk ivory was also a popular material for American canes, as seen in the phrenology head example (b). Popular in the nineteenth century, the theory of phrenology maintained that the shape of a person's skull determined his or her character and aptitude. Accordingly, the precise location of cranial bumps and valleys, as mapped out on such heads as shown here, revealed an individual's relative strength and weakness in specific human characteristics, such as "order," "wit," and "individuality." Such phrenology canes provided a variation on the longstanding tradition of using heads to surmount canes. A logical termination for a cane's vertical shaft, a head also provided sculptural interest and could comfortably fit the hand.

One of the many genres in which this collection excels is the nautical, or scrimshaw, cane, which was traditionally made by sailors from such maritime materials as whale bone, baleen, narwhal, and walrus tusk (see examples c–e). They were often crafted to fill the long hours at sea. The shaft of the cane with the bird handle in this group (c) is wrapped with a veneer of baleen, a hornlike material from the upper jaws of certain whales that was also used to make corset stays. The virtuosic architectural cane with twisted columns (d) is topped

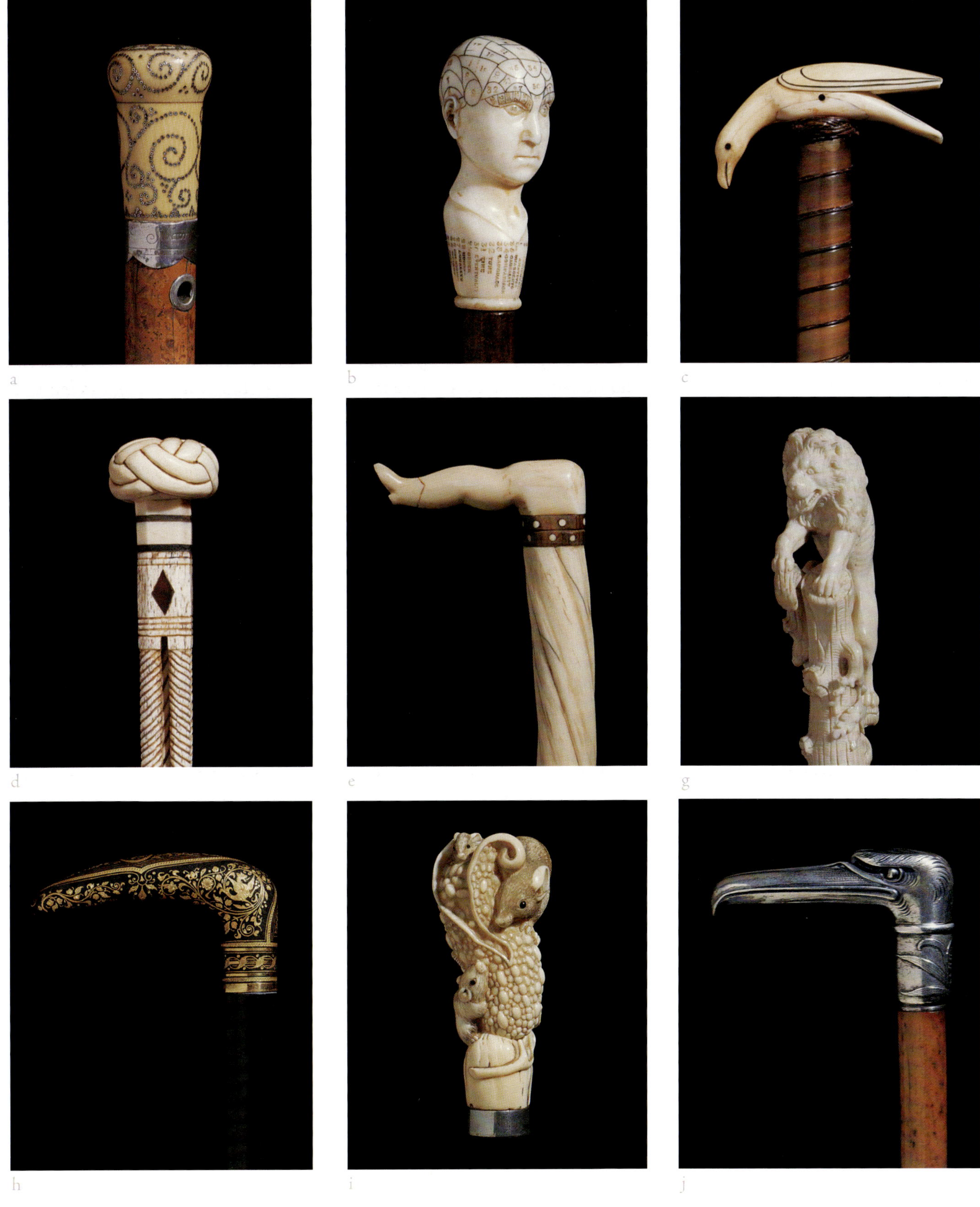

a b c

d e g

h i j

f) Attributed to Michael Cribbins (Mike/Orion), American, 1839–1917
Cane
1861
Polychrome and gilt on diamond willow
L: 35 in.
Carved inscription in relief: MIKE/WAR/1861

g) German, unidentified maker
Cane (male lion in a tree)
ca. 1870
Elephant ivory handle, ebonized hardwood shaft, horn ferrule
L: 36 in.

h) Probably Spanish, unidentified maker
Damascene cane
ca. 1890
Gold on oxidized steel handle, maccassar ebony shaft, replaced brass ferrule
L: 38¼ in.

i) American with imported Japanese handle
Cane (mouse family eating squash)
ca. 1890
Elephant ivory handle, ebony shaft, horn ferrule
L: 34¼ in.

j) Tiffany and Company, American
Cane with Thomas Nast eagle handle
ca. 1890
Silver handle, malacca shaft, horn ferrule
L: 35 in.
Marked: Tiffany and Co. Maker, Sterling

with a common motif, the so-called Turk's-head knot, which was a decorative and functional knot often used aboard ships. Narwhal, which forms the shaft of the cane with the popular lady's leg handle (e), is the spiral-shaped tusk from a narwhal, a small type of arctic whale. In centuries past, the rare narwhal tusks were thought to perhaps come from the legendary unicorn and were especially valued. A male cane owner no doubt experienced a degree of titillation by clasping a handle in the shape of a lady's leg. This handle type was one of the milder, more socially acceptable forms of erotic or "naughty" canes, which often featured more sexually explicit imagery.

Many canes in this collection date from the late nineteenth and early twentieth centuries, when canes enjoyed their heyday as fashion accessories and presentation pieces. The elaborately etched cane depicting "Heroes of the U.S. Navy" (l) was presented in 1900 to Henry John Heinz, the founder of Heinz ketchup, by John Bindley, a Pittsburgh hardware magnate who later became the president of Pittsburgh Steel. Luxury canes for the upper classes sported an enlarged array of handle materials including damascene (h), glass, porcelain, obsidian, silver, and gold. Elaborately carved ivory handles imported from Japan (i) became more available as well and satisfied the widespread Victorian taste for virtuosic carving and vivid realism. The eagle head for the ca. 1890 Tiffany cane (j) originated in a design by Thomas Nast, the famed late-nineteenth-century American illustrator and political cartoonist. Confirming the source, Tiffany sent Nast a complimentary eagle cane with a note that stated in part, "Doubtlessly you will recognize the Nast Eagle."

Several of the folk canes in this collection capitalize on the unique features of their carefully selected materials. In the case of the cane (f) by Mike/Orion (identified as Michael Cribbins, 1839–1917, from Michigan), the painted and carved decoration accentuates the irregularities of the diamond willow, a strong, lightweight wood of the Upper Midwest that forms diamond-shaped blisters after its branches are infected by a fungus. Dating this cane "1861" and inscribing in raised gold letters "War," the maker clearly had some appreciation for the historical significance of the Civil War, which had just begun. The maker of the elegant spiraling wooden cane (k) transformed a piece of curving vine-strangled burl into a serpent by carving scales into the surface and applying glass eyes. By contrast, the wooden cane by "Schnider" (m), probably made in the south, is carved from top to bottom with a menagerie of animals associated with warmer climates. Here a large snake and alligator try to swallow a dog, whose collar bears the maker's name.

Through their artistry and varied social functions, canes provide an illuminating window onto the taste, social mores, and aesthetic preferences of the times in which they were made and used.

BJM

k) American, unidentified maker
Cane
ca. 1890
Hand-carved burl wood handle, snake with yellow glass, brass collar, vine-strangled hardwood shaft, yellow glass, white metal and iron ferrule
L: 36 in.

l) American, unidentified maker
Cane
ca. 1900
Etched birch
L: 34¾ in.
Inscribed: John Bindley / to / H. J. Heinz / Nov. 1900; Heroes of the U.S. Navy . . .

m) "Schnider," American, dates unknown
Cane
ca. 1910
High-relief carved animals
Hardwood shaft, brass and iron ferrule
L: 36 in.

Dike, Catherine. *Canes in the United States: Illustrated Mementoes of American History, 1607–1953*. Ladue, MO: Cane Curiosa Press, 1994.

Klever, Ulrich. *Walkingsticks: Accessory, Tool, and Symbol*. Atglen, PA: Schiffer Publishing, 1996.

Snyder, Jeffrey B. *Canes from the Seventeenth to the Twentieth Century*. Atglen, PA: Schiffer Publishing, 1993.

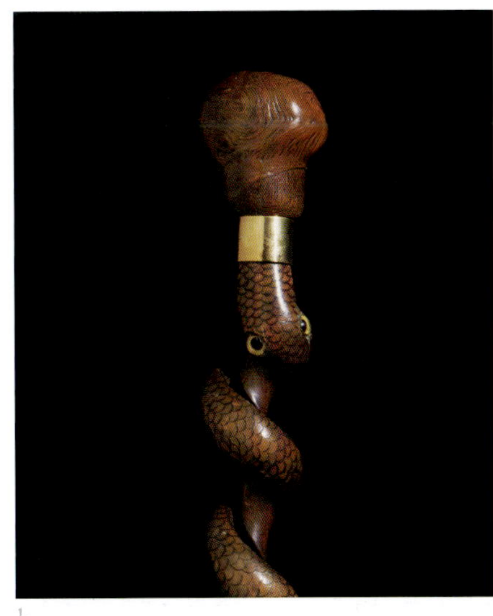
k

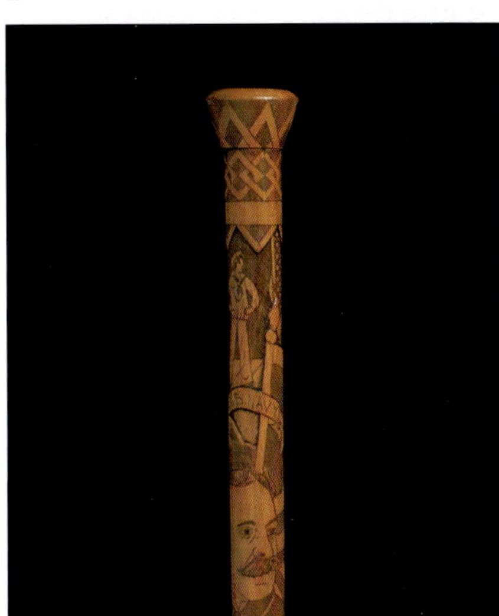
l

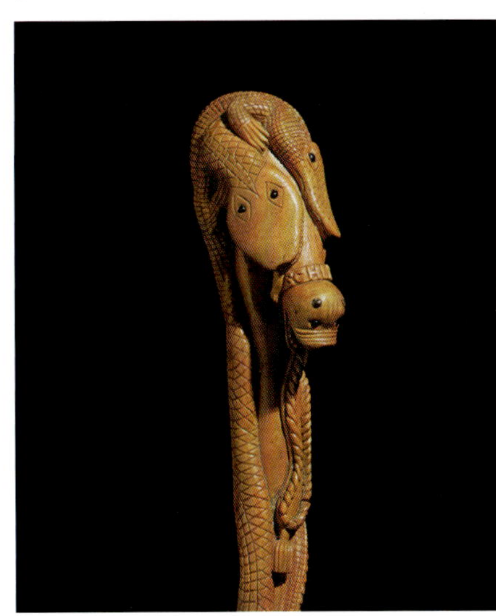
m

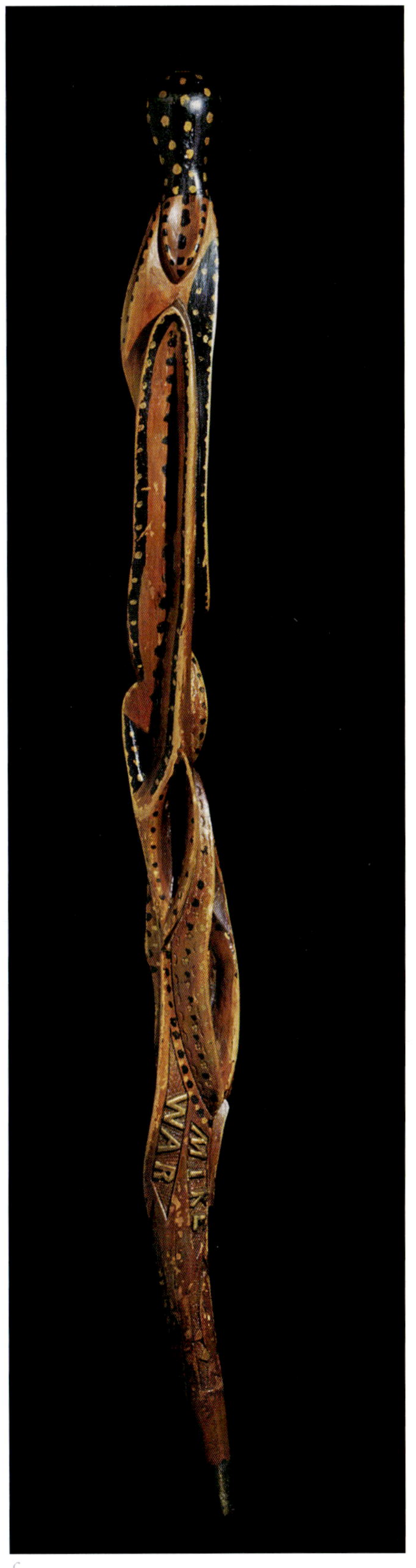

f

3 Unknown artist, Yoruba peoples, Nigeria

Figures

19th century
Wood, cowrie shells, hide, and fiber
H: 22½ in.

Partial gift of Valerie Franklin in honor of Tamara Northern and partial purchase through the Mrs. Harvey P. Hood W'18 Fund

In Yoruba religion, Eshu-Elegba—commonly referred to as Eshu—is the trickster deity who embodies the principles of unpredictability, opposition, and contradiction. Eshu, who is also the messenger between the creator god, lesser deities, and humans, has a dual character: wild and orderly, male and female, young and old. Many Yoruba folktales tell of Eshu's cunning ability to outwit unsuspecting victims by playing tricks that deal out vital lessons about straddling the seam between two different perspectives.

In Yoruba religious sculpture, the physical features on an object often provide visual clues to the characteristics and powers of a particular deity. The more prominent the physical feature, the more important its symbolic or conceptual meaning. In Yoruba sculpture, Eshu may be represented as either male or female, as epitomized in this ensemble of four joined staffs made up of two female figures framed by a male figure on each side. Both females hold their breasts, displaying the gesture of obeisance required of female devotees. The male figures hold a medicine gourd in each hand, a characteristic of Yoruba religious sculpture in which sacred representations carry objects in their hands to identify their powers. The medicine gourds symbolize Eshu's powerful and beguiling influence over humans—an influence that can work for or against a person, depending upon his or her outlook on life.

The four figures all wear Eshu's characteristically pointed, phallic hairstyle to emphasize and reflect upon his notorious conceit, sexuality, and strength. Suspended from the figures are strands of cowrie shells, once used as currency in most of Africa, which allude to the importance of Eshu in the marketplace, where there is great potential for conflict and where this trickster deity resides as guardian over monetary transactions. The contrast of these white shells against the dark wood further evokes Eshu and his contradictory nature.

BT

Fagg, William Buller, John Pemberton, and Bruce Holcombe. *Yoruba: Sculpture of West Africa.* New York: Knopf, 1982.

Westcott, Jean. "The Sculpture and Myths of Eshu-Elegba, the Yoruba Trickster: Definition and Interpretation in Yoruba Iconography." *Africa* 32:4 (October 1962): 336–53.

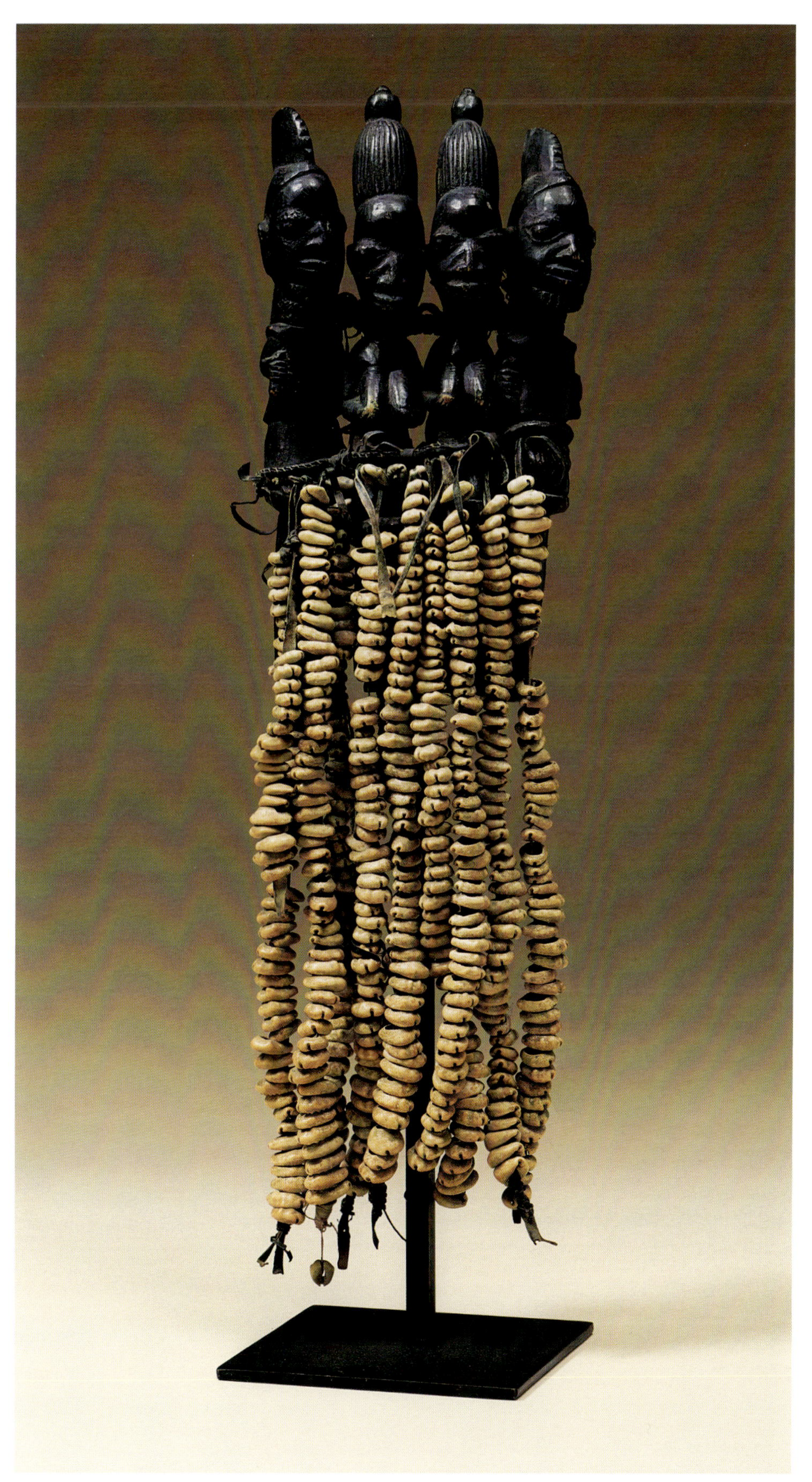

4 **JAMES HENRY CAFFERTY**

American, 1819–1869

Preparing to Fish

ca. 1846

Oil on canvas

16 x 12 in.

Gift of Frank P. Stetz in memory of David Stewart Hull, Class of 1960

James Henry Cafferty moved from Albany, New York, to New York City in 1839, and he was described as a sign painter in the city directories for 1839–40 and 1840–41. It seems that his only formal training as an artist consisted of two courses in the National Academy of Design's antique division that he attended beginning in 1841, but by 1843, when he exhibited a painting for the first time at the National Academy's exhibition, he was evidently a practicing artist. Despite his lack of academic training, Cafferty's work came to be respected by his peers—by 1850 he was elected an associate of the National Academy, and he was made a full Academician in 1853.

Cafferty produced *Preparing to Fish* early in his career, when he was working in a tight, linear manner that greatly differs from his late, more painterly, style (Williams 1973: 176). Interestingly, in terms of the subject, he would eventually become best known for his realistic paintings of fish. The painting was purchased in 1846 by the American Art Union, a subscription organization that sought to promote American artists by distributing their work to its members, and subsequently included in their annual lottery. As such, we can be assured that it was not intended as a portrait for a specific patron but as a rural genre scene. The two older boys in the foreground of the picturesque country setting are actively preparing to fish—one boy sits on a log with the bait in his lap, while the standing boy attaches the bait to the line. The younger boy in the background holds a bowl (perhaps containing food for the lamb), his hat resting behind him. In this painting, we can detect the influence of changing views on childhood. As opposed to the earlier Puritan notion that children were born into sin, the romantics, in the early nineteenth century, insisted on the child's innate goodness and closeness to heaven. Picturing children with animals and within the natural world was one way for artists to suggest their intimacy with God, through his creations. Cafferty's choice of a lamb further highlights the young boy's docility and innocence. In this idyllic scene, the children enjoy nature through relaxed and playful activities that would have perhaps inspired nostalgic memories for Cafferty's New York City audience.

MWL

Hull, David Stewart. *James Henry Cafferty, N.A. (1819–1869)*. New York: New-York Historical Society, 1986.

Humm, Rosamond Olmsted. *Children in America: A Study of Images and Attitudes*. Atlanta, GA: High Museum of Art, 1978.

Williams Jr., Hermann Warner. *Mirror to the American Past: A Survey of American Genre Painting: 1750–1900*. Greenwich, CT: New York Graphic Society, 1973.

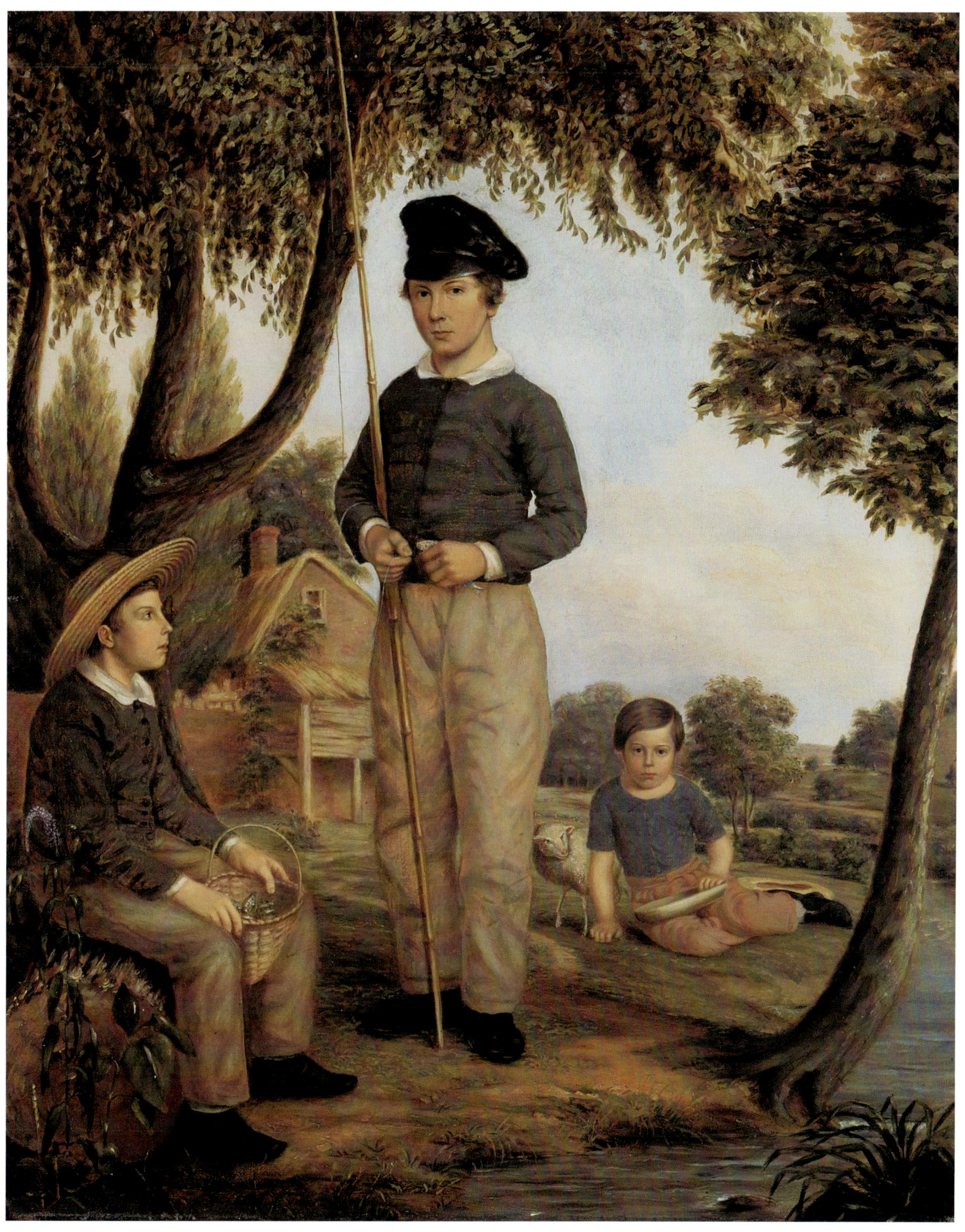

5 **FÉLIX TEYNARD**

French, 1817–1892

General View Taken from Point I on the Roof Terrace of the First Pylon Island of Fila (Philae)

ca. 1851
Salted paper print from a calotype negative
9½ x 12 in.

Gift of Harley and Stephen C. Osman, Class of 1956, Tuck 1957

Félix Teynard was trained as a civil engineer, but he chose to leave this career in 1842 to pursue the new technology of photography. With no commission and no specific knowledge of Egyptology, he traveled to Egypt in 1851 and used the recently invented calotype technique to document the region's buildings, ruins, landscape, and people. Henry Fox Talbot developed the calotype in 1840 and publicly introduced it in mid-1841. In calotype, the photographer exposed a chemically treated sheet of high quality drawing paper to a scene using a camera, and a latent, or invisible, image formed on it. In a darkened room, the addition of more chemicals developed a visible negative image of the original scene. Multiple prints could then be made from this negative through the salt print process. In this process, also invented by Talbot, a piece of printing paper was soaked in a solution of gelatin and salts, dried, and then brushed with a solution of silver nitrate. The paper was then placed under the negative, fixed under glass, and exposed to sunlight. The result was a brown-toned image like the one here. Teynard clearly mastered the process, as his calotypes are possibly the most technically perfect examples that exist.

Upon Teynard's return to France, over 160 of his calotypes were exhibited in 1855 in Paris and subsequently published in 1858 in an album titled *Egypte et Nubie: Sites et monuments les plus intéressants pour l'étude de l'art et de l'histoire* (Egypt and Nubia: The most interesting sites and monuments for the study of art and history). This particular calotype was taken on the famous island of Philae, which was the center for the worship of the goddess Isis during the Ptolemaic era of Egyptian history. Philae was covered in temples, courts, and colonnades mostly constructed between 285 and 246 BCE. Teynard's shot looks out along what is now known as the "West Colonnade" on the right and the "East Unfinished Colonnade" on the left. Philae was flooded each year from December to April until the construction of the Aswan dam in the 1970s. Because the dam was going to cause the island to be permanently submerged by Lake Nassar, a hugely ambitious project was undertaken to move all of the structures to the nearby island of Agilkia. Teynard's images of Philae provide a valuable record of the monuments and temples in their original locations.

MWL

Howe, Kathleen Stewart. *Félix Teynard: Calotypes of Egypt: A Catalogue Raisonné.* New York: H. P. Kraus, 1992.

Jammes, André, and E. Parry-Janis. *The Art of French Calotype.* Princeton: Princeton University Press, 1983.

Jammes, André, and Marie-Thérèse Jammes. *En Egypte au temps de Flaubert: les Premiers Photographes, 1839–1860.* Paris: Kodak Pathé, 1976.

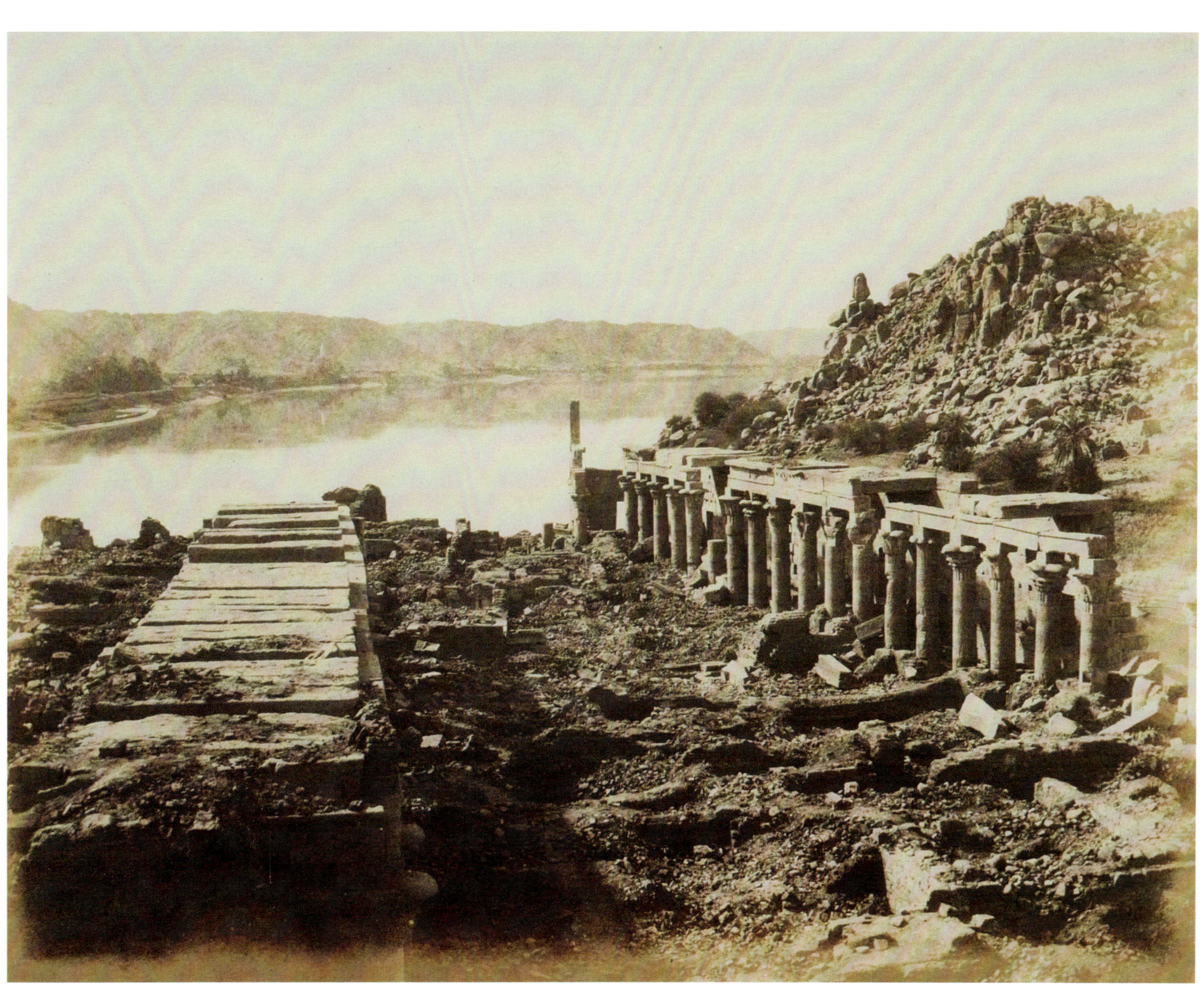

6 **EUGÈNE CICERI**
French, 1813–1890

Stone Quarry in the Environs of Paris

1855–60
Watercolor and gouache on paper
8⅞ x 12⅜ in.

Promised gift of Patricia Hewitt and Dale C. Christensen Jr., Class of 1969

Photograph by Bruce M. White

In this work, the foreground depicts a number of workers and supervisors laboring at a quarry on the outskirts of Paris. The city's skyline is visible in the distance. The bleak environment—without any vegetation, structures, or transportation equipment—seems to accentuate the difficulty of the task. Moreover, the relatively low horizon enhances the effects of the dramatic lighting and austere atmosphere.

Eugène Ciceri worked as a painter and lithographer in many genres, although he was mainly known as a landscapist. He first exhibited at the Salon of 1851 and often executed his compositions using techniques employed by contemporary Barbizon artists, such as Charles-François Daubigny, Narcisse Diaz de la Peña, and others. In addition, he largely embraced the focus of these artists on unidealized views, usually natural scenes and subjects from everyday life.

The artist's portrayal of the quarry represents an important moment in the history of the rebuilding of Paris. The capital city shown in the background underwent an enormous renewal program between 1852 and 1870 in an effort to alleviate overcrowded housing, serious health problems, and other deplorable urban conditions. The new stone-lined boulevards stretched for miles across old neighborhoods and recently annexed suburban districts. The new water and sewer systems, monumental buildings, and other improvements required considerable materials, especially limestone. However, while the massive reconstruction scheme was aimed at modernizing Paris, Ciceri's image indicated that the operation relied mostly on manual technology. Consequently, the artist's contemporary interest in routine settings and activities led to unexpected insights into the complexities involved in updating a city still based largely on an artisanal and unskilled workforce.

TBT

Daguerre de Hureaux, Alain. "Eugène Ciceri." *Grove Art Online*, Oxford University Press. http://www.groveart.com

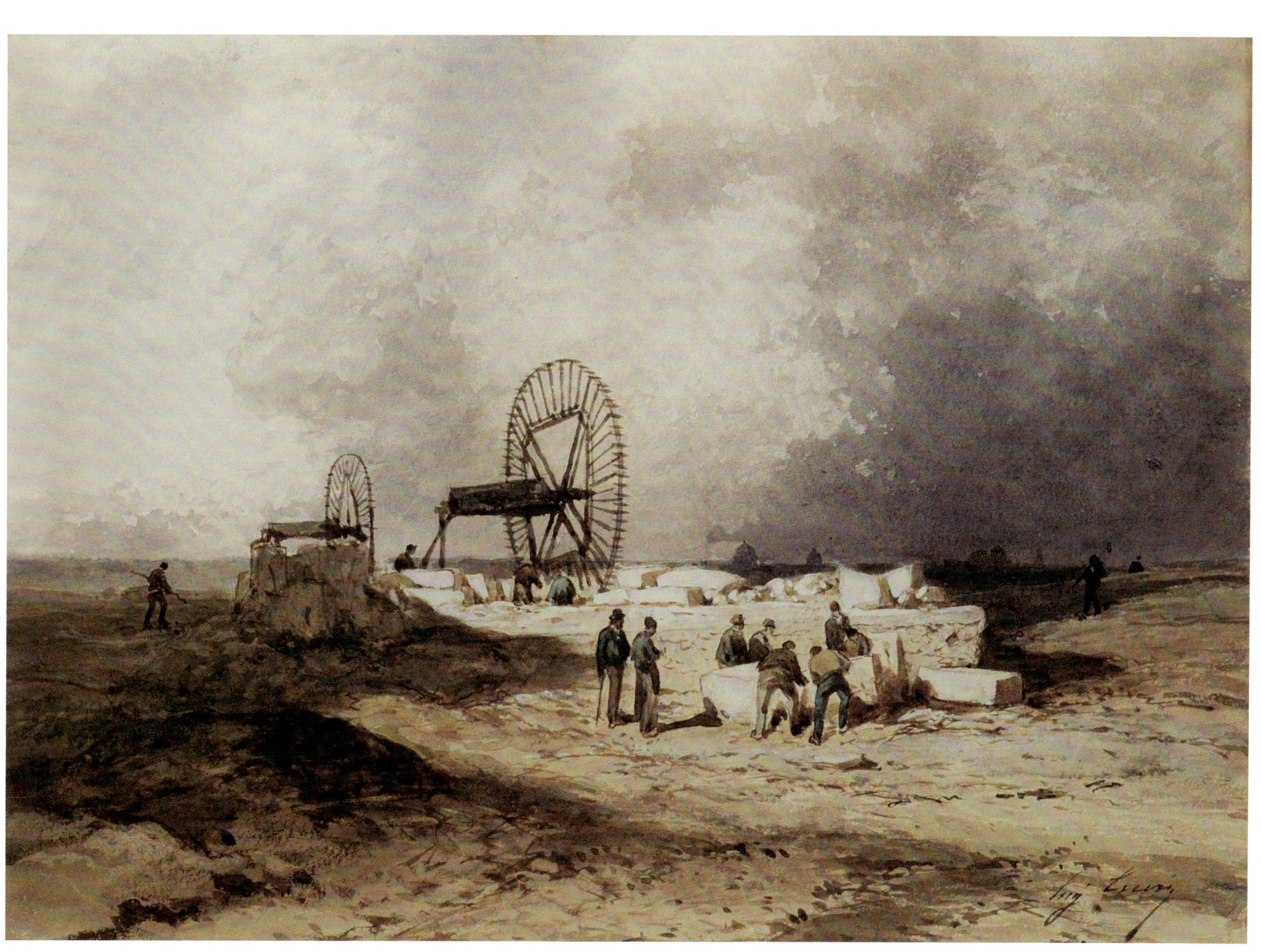

7 JESSE TALBOT

American, 1806–1879

White Mountain Landscape

1856
Oil on canvas
22 x 27 in. (oval)

Gift of Catherine Dail Weil, Class of 1985, in memory of her father, Lewis Dail, Class of 1956

In this radiant landscape Jesse Talbot suggests both the physical beauty and the symbolic potency of New Hampshire's White Mountains, one of the nation's most revered wilderness areas. By 1856, when Talbot painted this composition, the White Mountains were easily accessible by rail or coach, and numerous grand hotels hosted thousands of visitors from Boston and New York who were eager to experience the region's picturesque scenery and bracing fresh air. This painting, however, accentuates the idea of the White Mountains in the popular imagination rather than the region's contemporary status as a burgeoning tourist destination. Talbot depicts in the distance the distinctive silhouette of the highest peak in the northeast, Mount Washington, and situates it in an expansive, verdant, almost primordial landscape, that has little basis in the actual topography of New Hampshire. The centrally placed, life-sustaining waterfall and calm lake recall eighteenth-century landscape conventions as well as several specific works by Thomas Cole, Talbot's influential Hudson River school predecessor. Here, however, a brilliant sunset bathes the scene in a warm glow that reveals Talbot's expertise with atmospheric effects as well as the more recent advent of the luminist aesthetic in American landscape painting. The painting's tondo, or rounded, framing—a format especially associated with late Renaissance religious paintings—distances this scene further from the workaday world and reinforces the long-held association of the New World's wilderness with Eden and with God's immanent presence in nature.

Born in the first decade of the nineteenth century, Jesse Talbot began exhibiting at the National Academy of Design in New York in 1838 and continued to do so until 1860. He was elected an associate member of the academy in 1842 or 1843. He also exhibited at other New York venues, including the Apollo Association and the Brooklyn Art Association. In addition to the White Mountains, he traveled to the Catskills, the Adirondacks, the Cumberland Valley, and Vermont in search of landscape subjects.

BJM

Campbell, Catherine H. *New Hampshire Scenery: A Dictionary of Nineteenth Century Artists of New Hampshire Mountain Landscapes*. Canaan, NH: Phoenix Publishing, for the New Hampshire Historical Society, 1985.

McGrath, Robert L. *Gods in Granite: The Art of the White Mountains of New Hampshire*. Syracuse, NY: Syracuse University Press, 2001.

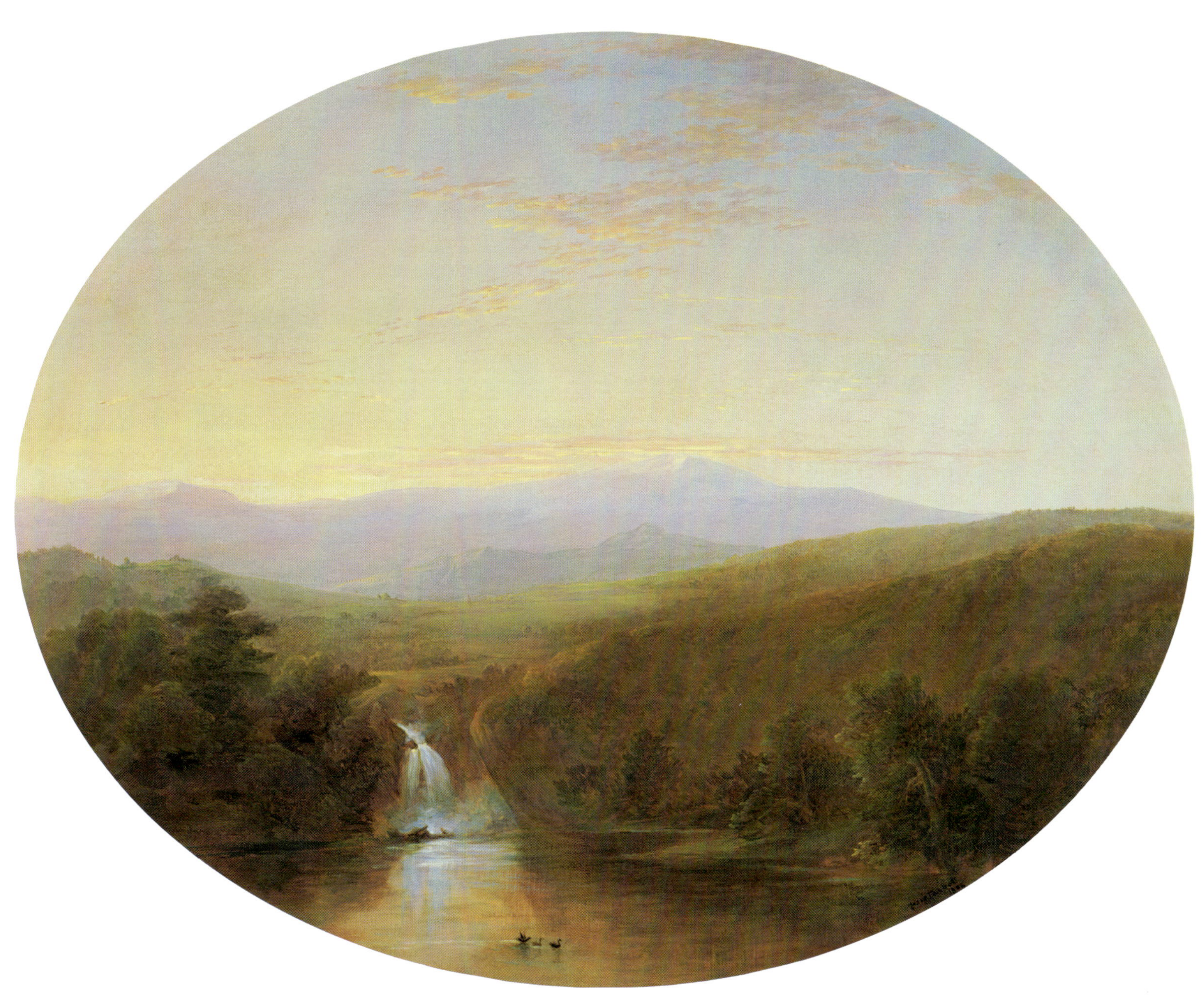

8 **JOHN ADAMS PARKER**

American, 1827–ca. 1905

Autumn in the Adirondacks

ca. 1860
Oil on canvas
14 x 24 in.

Promised gift of Dr. Michel Hersen and Victoria Jenkins Hersen, in memory of Gordon Milo Jenkins, Class of 1926

Relatively little is known of John Adams Parker, a Brooklyn-based landscape painter active from the late 1850s through the late nineteenth century. He graduated from New York University and worked as a merchant in the early 1850s before turning to the study of painting. In 1864 he was named an associate member of the National Academy of Design, where he exhibited from 1858 to 1886. He also exhibited at the Brooklyn Art Association from 1861 to 1886, among other venues. It is clear from the titles of his works that Parker, like many landscape artists based in New York, made frequent painting excursions to the Adirondacks, the Catskills, and the White Mountains. Early in his career he painted luminous landscapes rendered in a tight, realist manner, while later he favored intimate, twilight subjects that revealed a more poetic approach to nature that was consistent with tonalism.

Like many of Parker's early works, *Autumn in the Adirondacks* celebrates the scenic beauty of undeveloped regions north of New York City. In its horizontal format, serene subject, and attention to an enveloping, radiant light, the work reflects the luminist style of Parker's better-known contemporaries Martin Johnson Heade and John Frederick Kensett. His careful elaboration of every leaf and every ripple of water, however, also aligns him with the Pre-Raphaelite aesthetic, which privileged highly particularized detail. The work adheres to compositional formulas long associated with landscape painting, such as the use of framing elements, a body of water that leads the viewer's eye toward the horizon, and a progressively more atmospheric treatment of receding landscape features. In the hands of an earlier generation of romantic landscapists certain details, such as the barren limbs in the right foreground, would have served as ominous reminders of nature's more tempestuous moods. Parker, however, portrays the lifeless trees with a convincing, matter-of-fact realism. Their sharp silhouettes add graphic interest without detracting from the painting's portrayal of the region as an unspoiled, yet welcoming, destination for tourists eager to escape their urban confines.

BJM

Falk, Peter Hastings. *Who Was Who in American Art, 1564–1975: 400 Years of Artists in America*. Madison, CT: Sound View Press, 1999.

Kloss, William. *This Tranquil Land: Hudson River Paintings from the Hersen Collection*. Seattle: Frye Art Museum, 2000.

Naylor, Maria. *The National Academy of Design Exhibition Record, 1861–1900*. 2 vols. New York: Kennedy Galleries, 1973.

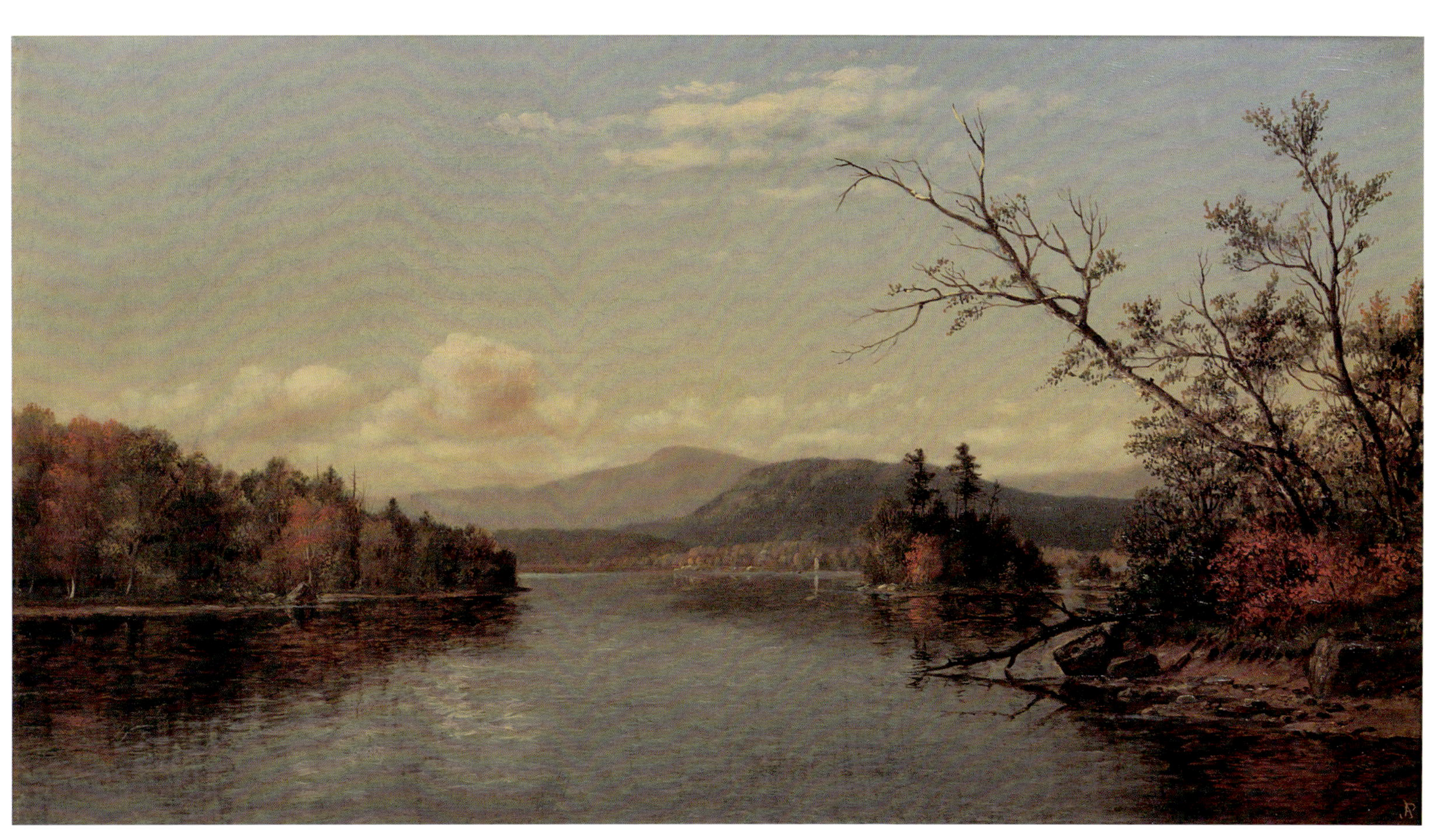

9 CHARLES-FRANÇOIS DAUBIGNY

French, 1817–1878

The Banks of the Oise River at Mériel

1867
Oil on panel
15 x 26½ in.

Promised gift of Patricia Hewitt and Dale C. Christensen Jr., Class of 1969

Photograph by Bruce M. White

This landscape represents a picturesque setting along the Oise River near the town of Mériel, north of Paris. The carefully juxtaposed strokes of unblended color and flickering light on the water reveal the artist's interest in capturing atmospheric effects. In addition, it appears to have been completed entirely *en plein air* ("in the open air") in the late evening during the summer. The emphasis on direct observation and spontaneous execution in order to capture the look of changing weather, times of day, and seasons formed a vision that inspired other artists to paint outdoors.

The Oise River was one of Charles-François Daubigny's favorite subjects. He moved to Auvers-sur-Oise in 1861 and remained there until his death in 1878. Traveling on a boat that had been converted into a studio, he continuously explored the surrounding waterways. Daubigny was evidently the first artist to paint his large works from nature. He was also one of the first to take an interest in the varying aspects of a particular scene, as well as in rendering these ephemeral effects with quick brushstrokes. These qualities placed Daubigny as an important figure in the development of a more naturalistic approach toward landscape painting, linking him to the impressionists, whose work he encouraged.

The interpretation of water, whether it was the sea, streams, rivers, pools, ponds, or lakes, was one of Daubigny's preferred themes. He was particularly adept at catching the shimmering appearance of light on water's surface, as well as the reflections of the sky and other features. At times he used a palette knife to apply the paint, employing a method later adapted by several impressionists. As a result, his subject matter, style, and technique marked a transition toward more modern forms of artistic expression.

TBT

Hellebranth, Robert. *Charles-François Daubigny, 1817–1878*. Morges: Matute, 1976. See esp. p. 63, no. 168.

Valuable Paintings from the Collection of the Late George F. Baker. Parke-Bernet Galleries, New York, 1938. See p. 34, no. 54.

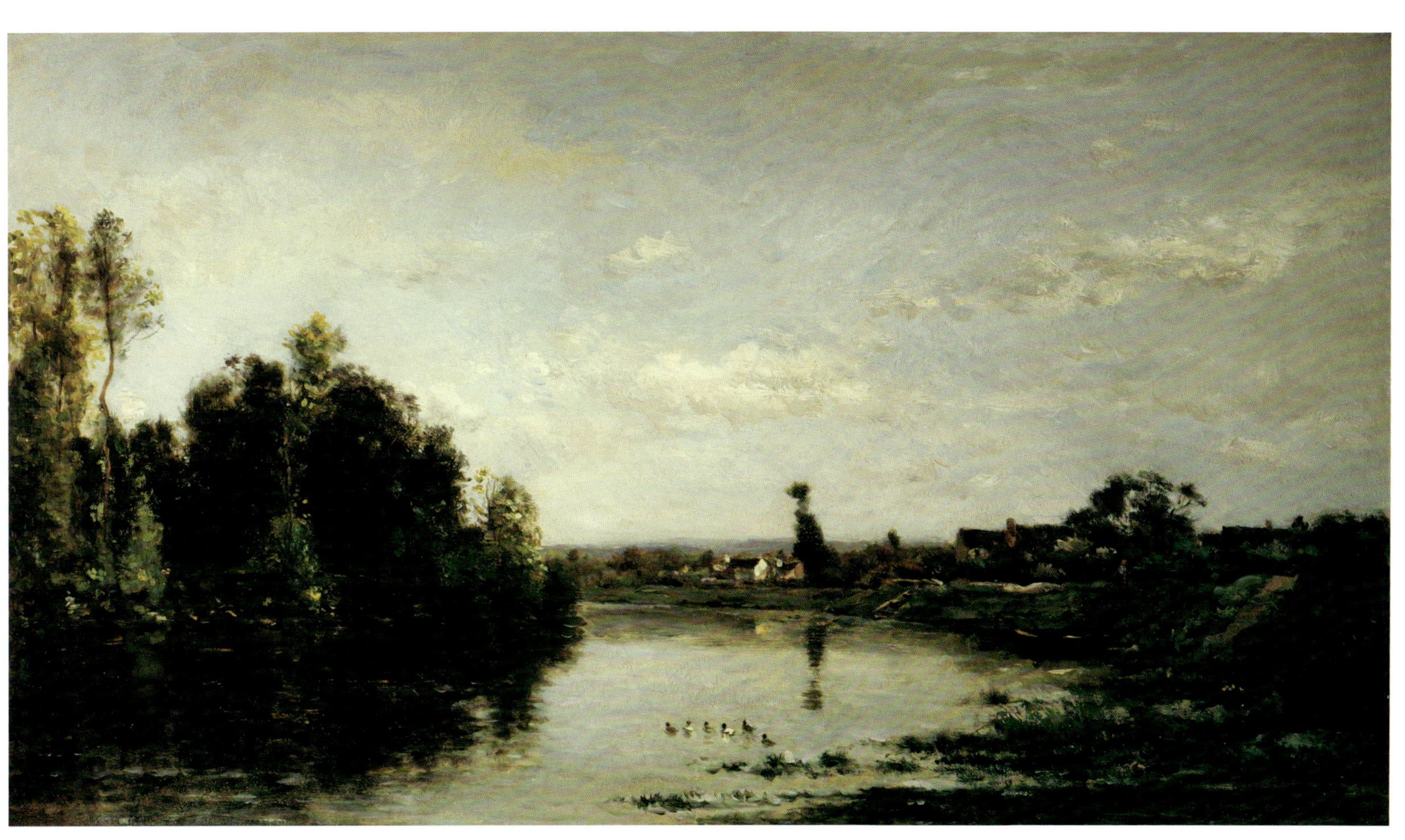

10 WILLIAM TROST RICHARDS

American, 1833–1905

Darmstadt

1867
Graphite on wove paper
8¾ x 12 in.

Gift of Ellen and Theodore Conant

William Trost Richards was one of the most gifted and prolific draftsmen of the nineteenth century. He began his career as a designer and illustrator of ornamental metalwork in Philadelphia in the early 1850s. Through studies with Paul Weber, a German immigrant landscape painter, Richards further honed his drawing skills, which he eagerly applied to his newfound passion for landscape. His inclination toward specificity of detail gained further encouragement in the late 1850s and early 1860s through his encounters with the treatises of British aesthetician John Ruskin, who urged landscapists to practice an absolute "truth to nature." Richards soon became one of the most extreme adherents to the Ruskinian, or Pre-Raphaelite, mode in this country. He especially mastered the art of rendering woodland scenes, in which he articulated every leaf, frond, and undulation of tree bark with equal deliberateness.

Richards drew this much more atmospheric drawing during an extended 1866–67 stay in Darmstadt, Germany, where he visited his friend and former teacher, Weber, who had returned to Germany in 1860. Particularly taken with the area's majestic oaks, Richards wrote to his patron George Whitney, "In the parks which have always been the property of the dukes & kings, the trees have become monarchs too, and I can not render the strange sense as of a dream with which I remember the old twisted oaks and the deer" (quoted in Ferber 1973: 30). In his work Richards accentuated the rough topography of the ancient tree trunk in the foreground with characteristic precision, but he sharply silhouetted its craggy branches against a diffusely rendered landscape. Gone is the artist's former predilection for uniform clarity of detail. He rendered the more distant trees with delicate, evanescent shadings that suggest a veil of mist partially obscuring their forms. Richards's sophisticated mix of drawing techniques gives the work a dreamlike quality that dramatizes all the more the anthropomorphic majesty of the noble tree in its mysterious, parklike setting.

BJM

Ferber, Linda. *William Trost Richards: American Landscape & Marine Painter, 1833–1905*. Brooklyn: The Brooklyn Museum, 1973.

Ferber, Linda. *William Trost Richards, Rediscovered: Oils, Watercolors, and Drawings from the Artist's Family*. New York: Beacon Hill Fine Art, 1997.

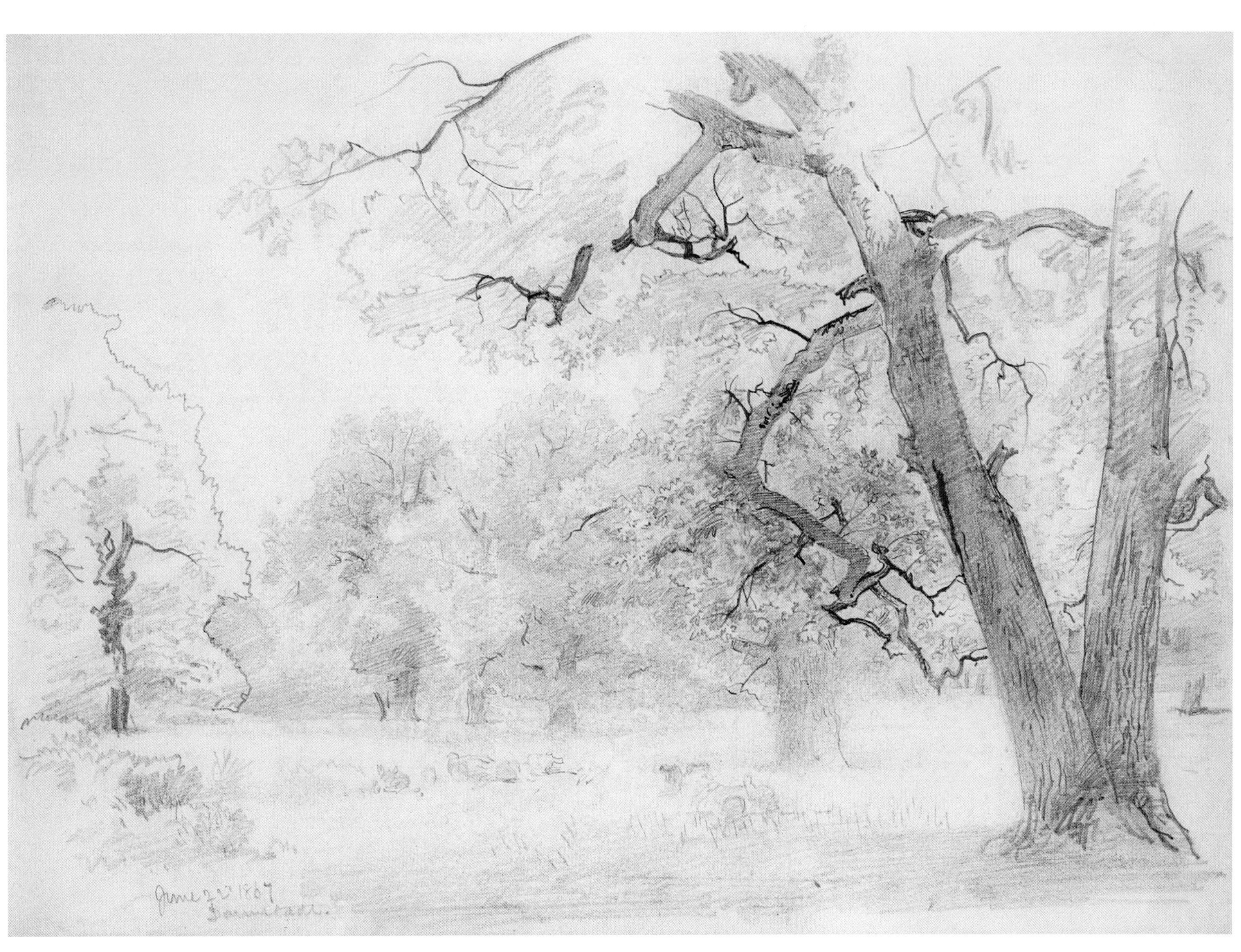
June 2d 1867

11 **DENNIS MILLER BUNKER**

American, 1861–1890

Sails and Nets Drying

ca. 1880–82
Oil on canvas
14½ x 21 in.

Gift of Jeffrey R. Brown, Class of 1961

This luminous oil sketch reveals the emerging and prodigious talent of Dennis Miller Bunker, whose brilliant painting career spanned just one decade, owing to his untimely death, apparently from cerebro-spinal meningitis. Although best known as an impressionist, Bunker varied his stylistic approach considerably during the 1880s. He began by painting nostalgic, rural landscapes and coastal subjects in a delicately tonal, preimpressionist style, as seen in this work. After honing his skills as a figure painter through studies in Paris from 1882 to 1885, he created several dark, meticulously modeled portraits and figural compositions in the academic tradition. He also pursued the rarefied beauty and mysterious, expressive tenor associated with the aesthetic movement, as evidenced by his evocative flower paintings and meditative portraits of elegant, fine-boned women silhouetted against dark backgrounds. After an influential summer in 1888 with John Singer Sargent in Calcot, England, Bunker added to his repertoire brilliant impressionist renderings of the marshes around Medfield, Massachusetts, and the greenhouse gardens of his Boston patron Isabella Stewart Gardner.

When Bunker painted this oil sketch in the early 1880s, he was fresh from studies at the Art Students League and the National Academy of Design, where he had been enrolled almost steadily from 1876 to 1882. At this time he fixed upon coastal subjects that he found on Long Island and especially Nantucket, where he spent childhood summers. His surviving paintings from this period almost invariably depict abandoned boats and fishing gear at low tide. As Erica Hirshler has noted, such images reflect the growing nostalgia for a simpler, preindustrial age in which mankind worked closely in tune with nature. Bunker shared this romantic impulse with many of his American contemporaries, including Winslow Homer, and with the mid-nineteenth-century Hague School and French Barbizon artists abroad. Unlike many of his counterparts on both sides of the Atlantic, however, he rarely included figures in these compositions. Here, the sunlit furled sails and suspended nets invoke, but do not depict, labor. Formally, they drape across the canvas like a rhythmic frieze, which is echoed in miniature by the broad, irregularly spaced strokes that animate the otherwise vacant foreground. The work's horizontal registers, punctuated by vertical accents, can be likened to musical notation itself—a fitting analogy for this music-loving artist. When Bunker painted this fresh, daringly modern oil sketch, he likely felt that it did not meet contemporary standards of finish and signed it, as he did his other oil studies, with prominent initials rather than the tidy, less conspicuous signature he appended to works intended for exhibition and sale. By the time the St. Botolph Club in Boston mounted his memorial exhibition in 1891, however, his peers felt quite otherwise and featured this work among a group of sixteen early sketches by the artist.

BJM

Hirshler, Erica E., with an essay by David Park Curry. *Dennis Miller Bunker: American Impressionist*. Boston: Museum of Fine Arts, Boston, 1994.

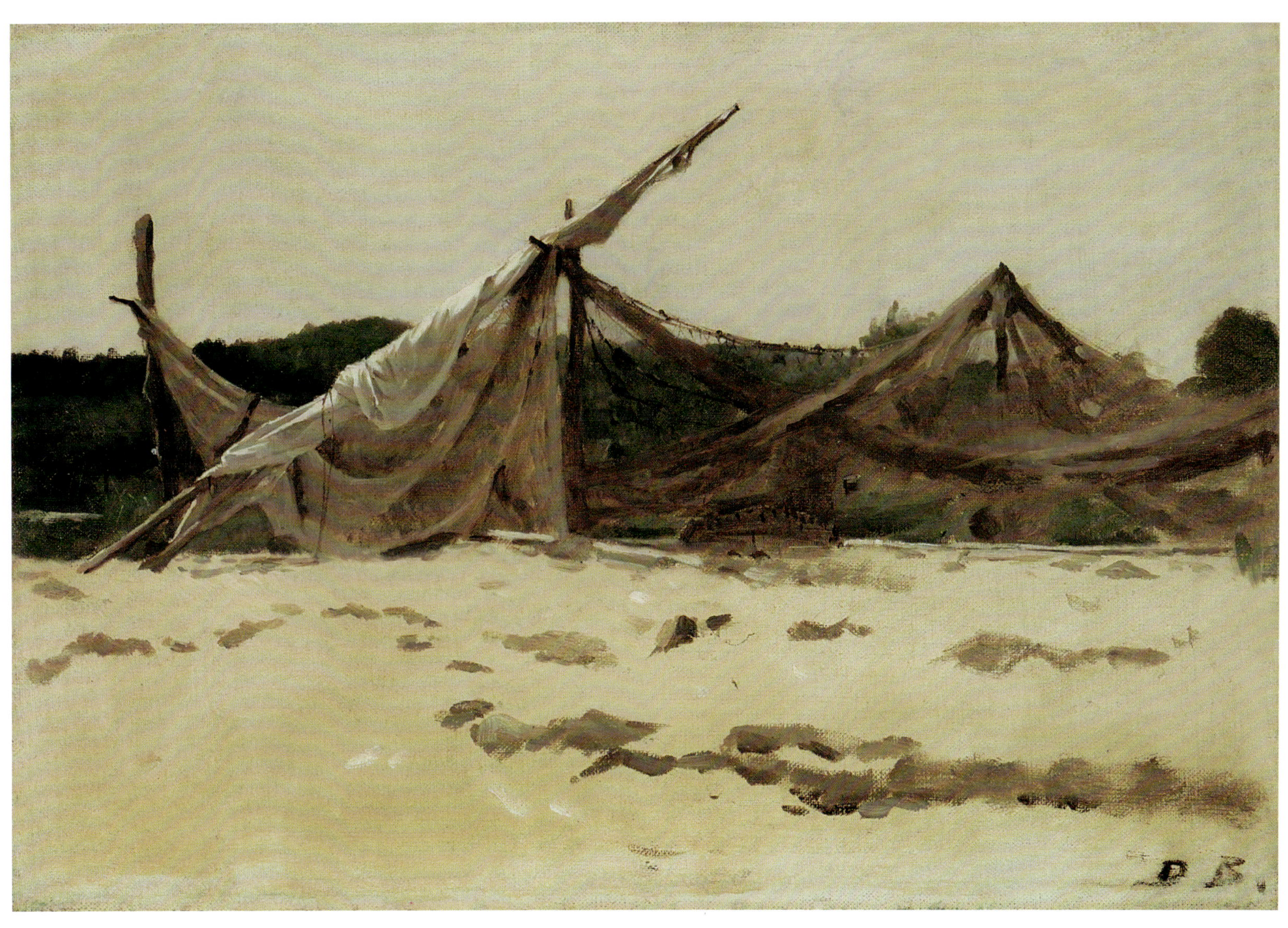

12 JAMES ENSOR

Belgian, 1860–1949

a) *Forest at Groenendael*

1888
Drypoint
4⅝ x 3⅛ in.

b) *The Gamblers*

1895
Etching
4⅝ x 6¼ in.

Promised gifts of Dr. David G. Stahl, Class of 1947

James Ensor is recognized, alongside Vincent Van Gogh and Edvard Munch, as a precursor of twentieth-century expressionism in his energetic use of line, and his creation of fantastic environments also influenced the surrealists. His most productive period was between 1880 and 1900. As a painter, his works were criticized or simply ignored at the exhibitions in Antwerp and Brussels in the 1880s. It was in 1886 that he began to produce the prints for which he would become best known, writing, "I want to survive, to speak for many years to the men of the future. I dream of solid copper, of indelible inks, of easy reproduction of images, and I therefore adopt etching as my chosen medium" (quoted in Croquez 1947: 8).

Forest at Groenendael presents the third and final state of this composition, which Ensor has signified by signing his name at the upper right corner. In the first state, the man at the center was the lone figure, creating a sense of foreboding solitude. However, by this last state, several other figures are present and even interacting. An underlying atmosphere of anxiety carries through Ensor's work and perhaps again finds expression here in the sinister twists and turns of the tree branches. He produced forty landscape prints over his career, mostly before 1889, and many of them demonstrated his interest in the effects of light in nature. Here, to produce the sense of bright light shining through a stand of trees, Ensor reduces trunks and branches to fine lines, with a single tree in the foreground standing out in dark silhouette.

The Gamblers is an example of Ensor's expressive, almost frenetic use of line to depict a strange, unsettling scene. The sketchy contours of the figures' bodies possess an energy that extends into their facial features. The ridiculousness of the central man's moustache is matched by the bulging eyes of a bearded figure at the left and the gruff, almost reptilian character of a man at the top right. At the card table, a gambler rests his head in his hand, out of fatigue or perhaps desperation, and stares out at the viewer. His body and face are rendered with a more distinct, bolder use of line than the other figures, and the contrast gives the circle of faces an almost hallucinatory quality. Ensor provides to the viewer a glimpse, perhaps, of the gambler's inner turmoil and anxiety as the world swirls around him.

MWL

Croquez, A. *L'Oeuvre gravé de James Ensor.* Geneva: P. Cailler, 1947.

Legrand, Francine-Claire. "James Ensor." *Grove Art Online.* Oxford University Press. http://www.groveart.com.

Taevernier, Aug. *James Ensor: Illustrated Catalogue of His Engravings, Their Critical Description, and Inventory of the Plates.* Ghent: N.V. Erasmus Ledeberg, 1973.

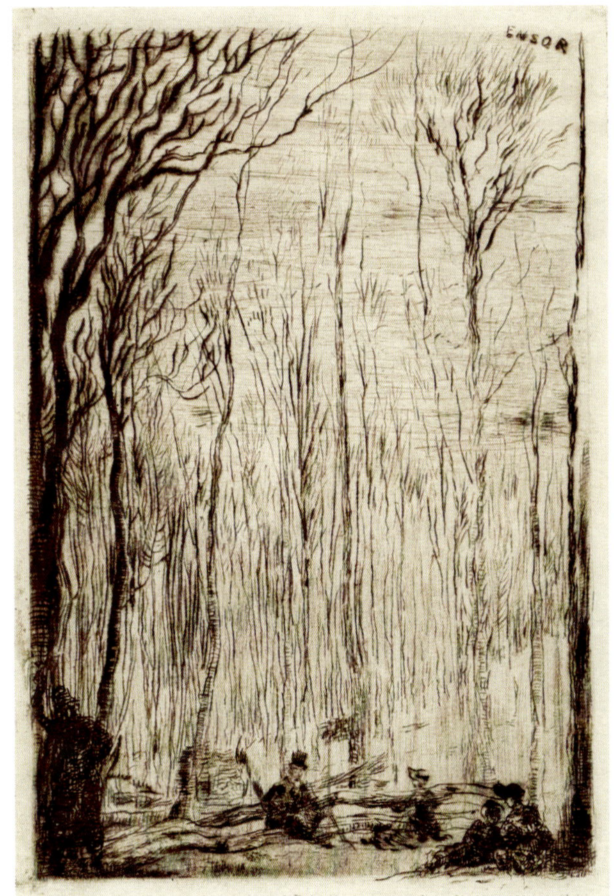

12 a

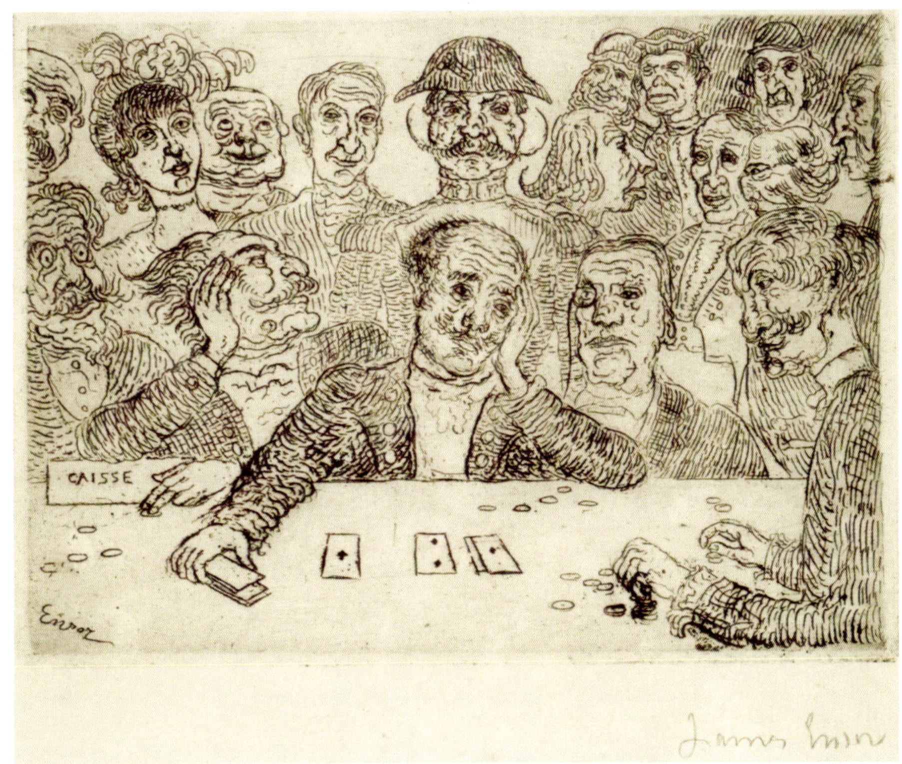

12 b

13 **J. ALDEN WEIR**

American, 1852–1919

Chrysanthemums

1888

Oil on canvas

12¾ x 18¼ in.

Promised gift of Jonathan L. Cohen, Class of 1960, Tuck 1961

J. Alden Weir painted this enchanting floral still life at an important transitional moment in his career, as he moved away from academic realism and toward more intimate, subjective compositions that reveal an awareness of vanguard approaches to painting. Weir had been well-grounded in the art of the past through studies at the National Academy of Design in New York and, in the mid-1870s, at the École des Beaux-Arts in Paris. Subsequent trips abroad in the early 1880s introduced him to alternative pictorial strategies through the works of such progressive figures as Edward Manet and James McNeill Whistler. Weir clearly looked to these and other contemporary influences as he forged his own manner in painting figural subjects, still lifes, and, beginning in the early 1890s, the outdoor impressionist landscapes for which he would become best known.

Painted in 1888, *Chrysanthemums* conveys an air of intimacy, restraint, and informality that contrasts with Weir's more conventional still lifes from the 1870s and early 1880s. The earlier works tended to depict tall, lavish bouquets of mixed blooms, displayed in elaborate containers centrally placed on the canvas. This composition, however, features a casual, closely cropped bouquet of white flowers, housed in a simple footed vessel situated to one side. Scattered sprigs and loose petals on the tablecloth balance the composition at left while alluding to the transient beauty of even the chrysanthemum, a sturdy garden staple. With a delicacy reminiscent of Whistler's tonal explorations, Weir renders the ostensibly white flowers with subtly modulated tints of white, cream, soft yellow, and gray. Spotlit against a dark, broadly painted background, the blooms emit a radiant glow and poetic aura. Weir's reverent portrayal recalls the elegiac, Asian-inspired floral still lifes of John La Farge and reminds us that for centuries flowers have alluded to life's ceaseless cycles of growth, maturity, death, and decay.

Weir's quest in the late 1880s for refined beauty and poetic suggestiveness through the floral still life aligns him with other American artists who painted flowers and were at that point associated with the aesthetic movement, including La Farge, Abbott Thayer, Dennis Miller Bunker, Emil Carlsen, William Merritt Chase, and Maria Oakey Dewing. Although Weir and Chase would soon turn to a more full-blown impressionism, all of these figures shared at this time a desire to create works that were artful yet seemingly uncontrived, deeply personal yet resonant with universal truths.

BJM

Burke, Doreen Bolger. *J. Alden Weir: An American Impressionist*. Newark: University of Delaware Press, 1983.

Foshay, Ella M. *Reflections of Nature: Flowers in American Art*. New York: Alfred A. Knopf, in association with the Whitney Museum of American Art, 1984.

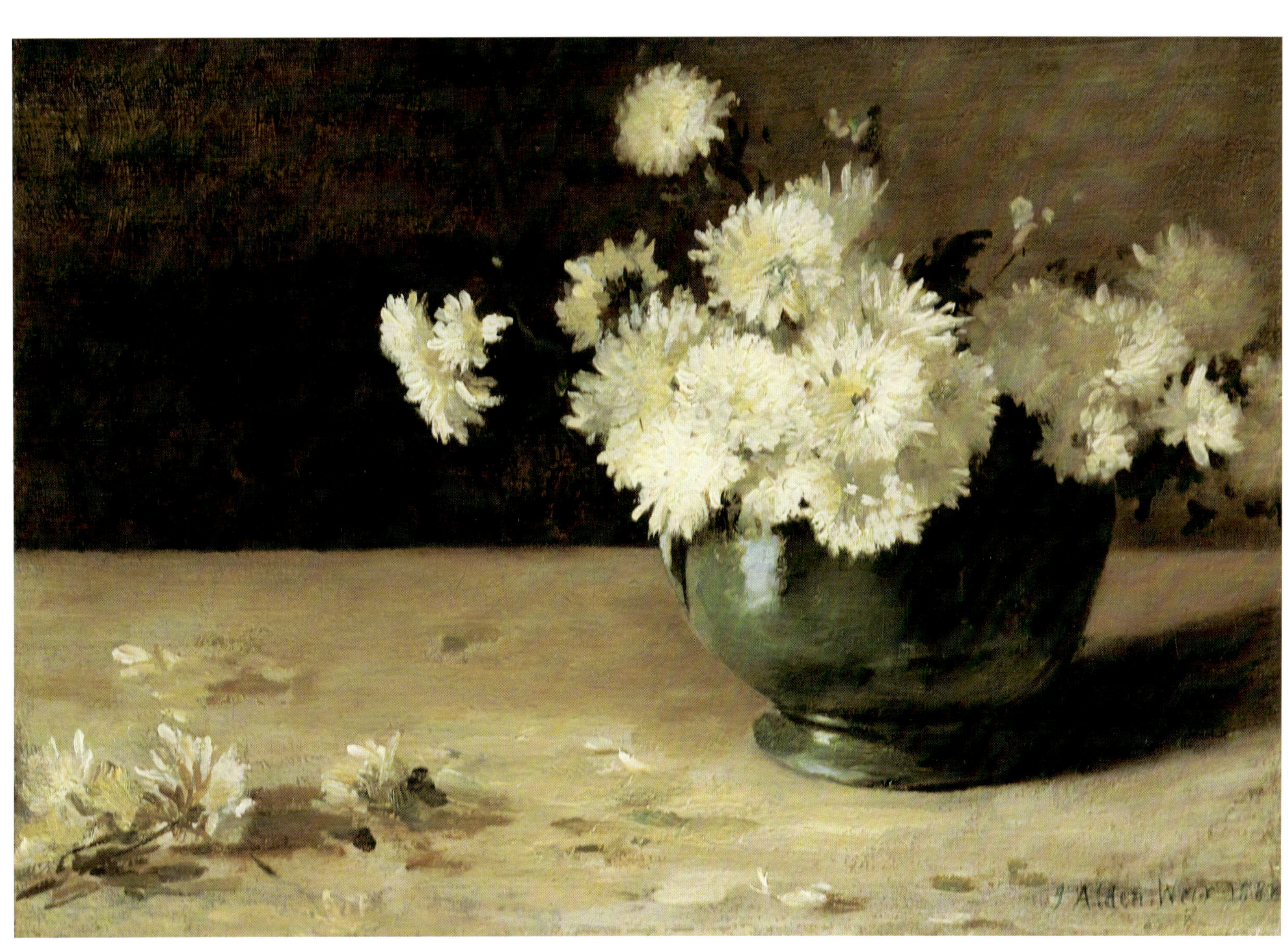

14 IRVING WILES

American, 1861–1948

Emily Henderson Cowperthwaite

1902
Oil on canvas
62 x 43 in.

Gift of Emily Henderson Graves Jones, granddaughter of the sitter

Irving Ramsey Wiles enjoyed a career as a successful society portraitist in the first decades of the twentieth century, working in a painterly style similar to that made popular by John Singer Sargent a decade earlier. Wiles had received his initial art training from his father, Lemuel Maynard Wiles, and then studied for a year at the Art Students League in New York City under Thomas Wilmer Dewing and William Merritt Chase. These instructors encouraged him to continue his training abroad in Paris, where he spent two years, primarily in the private studio of Carolus-Duran. Upon his return to America in 1884, while continuing his study, Wiles supplemented his income by producing illustrations for popular magazines. But in 1902, his career as a portraitist was secured—his painting of the famous actress Julia Marlowe was shown at the National Academy of Design exhibition and received overwhelming acclaim. Among the wealthy elite and art critics, Wiles came to be recognized as a portrait painter who could capture both the outer semblance and the true character of the sitter. His services were sought after by some of the most prominent and influential members of society.

Wiles painted this portrait in 1902, when Emily Henderson Cowperthwaite was twenty-five years old, as a wedding present for her and Walter Bernard Cowperthwaite, her new husband. His family had founded a successful Brooklyn furniture business, which he had relocated to Manhattan and continued to operate. The newlyweds became prominent figures in New York City society and on Long Island, where they also maintained homes. Wiles, who was a friend of Walter Cowperthwaite's parents, depicts Emily Cowperthwaite outdoors, surrounded by greenery, in a shimmering white dress embellished with lace. She holds a partially closed fan that highlights both her fashionability and her feminine modesty. Wiles renders Mrs. Cowperthwaite's face, neck, and shoulders very delicately, carefully blending his paint to suggest the smoothness of her skin. Within the dress, however, large expressive brushstrokes are visible that give a sense of immediacy and truthfulness, as if the portrait were taken on the spot, without any time for pretense. Wiles did experiment with impressionism in the landscapes and harbor scenes that he produced for his own pleasure, but otherwise he remained committed to traditional portraiture in the bold style that attracted so many patrons.

MWL

The Art of Irving Ramsey Wiles (1861–1948). With text by William D. Paul Jr. St. Joseph, MO: Albrecht Gallery, 1971.

Irving Ramsey Wiles, 1861–1948. With text by Nelson C. White. New York: Chapellier Galleries, 1967.

Reynolds, Gary A. *Irving R. Wiles*. New York: National Academy of Design, 1988.

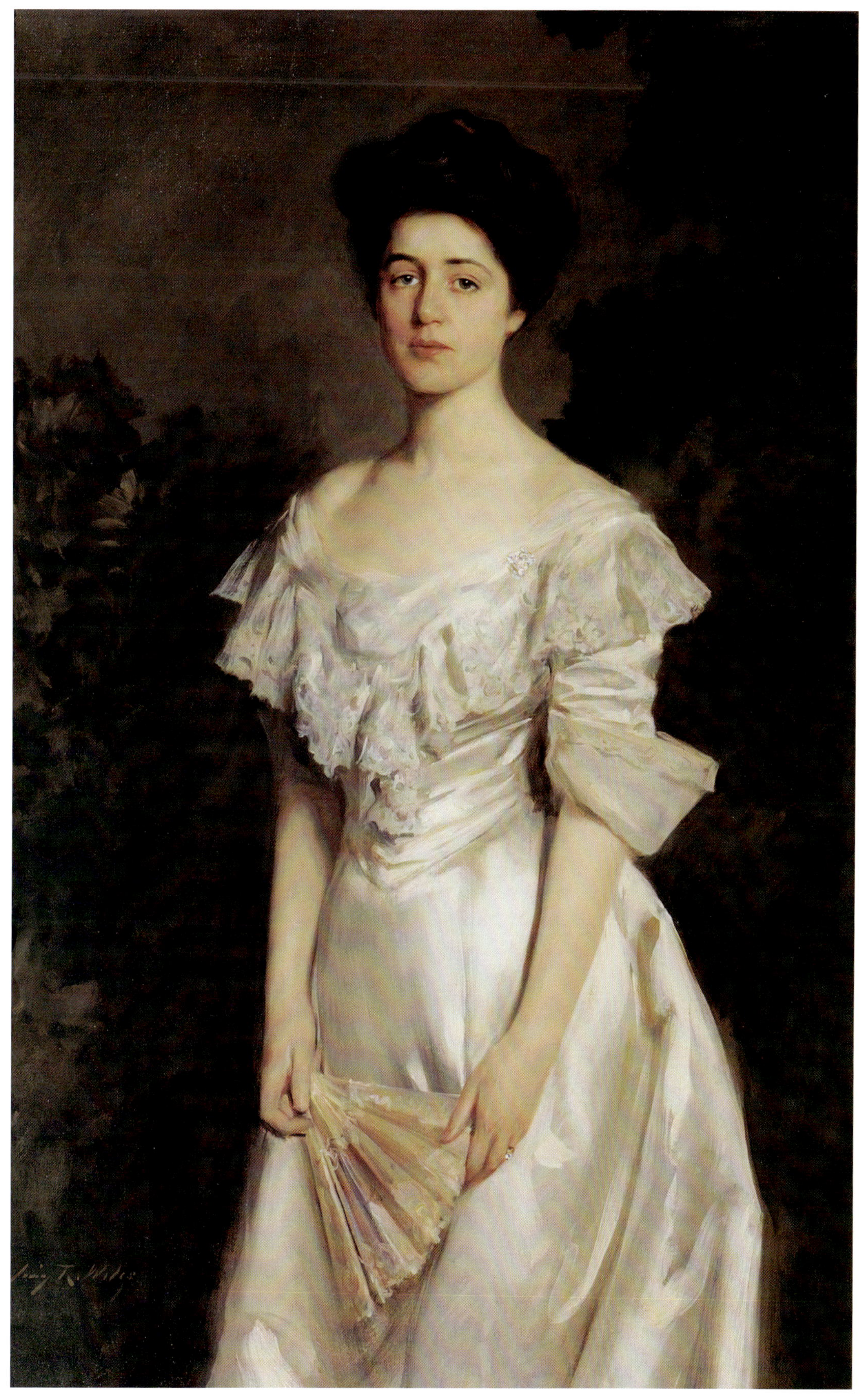

15 **GRUEBY FAIENCE COMPANY**

(1897–1909), American (Boston)
Designer: Addison B. LeBoutillier, 1872–1951

Tile (forest scene)

ca. 1906
Glazed earthenware
12⅛ x 11⅞ in.

Promised gift of William P. Curry, Class of 1957

At the turn of the twentieth century, the Boston art pottery firm of Grueby Faience Company, founded by William H. Grueby, gained international recognition for its velvety matte glazes in rich earth tones. In addition to a wide range of sturdy handthrown pottery vessels with organic forms and plant-inspired ornamentation, the company produced a variety of glazed architectural and decorative tiles. The most distinctive examples, of which this is one, were stylized pictorial tiles designed beginning around 1902 by Addison LeBoutillier, the firm's chief designer at that time. Most often used for fireplace surrounds and bathrooms, these tiles depicted landscapes, flowers, ships, animals, and medieval subjects such as knights and monks—all popular motifs associated with the broader arts and crafts style. This informal movement, which had its origins in England, rejected the recycled historical styles and machine-made household goods of the Victorian Age. It promoted instead an integration of the arts, handcraftsmanship, and simple ornamentation inspired by natural forms.

This large and impressive tile has long been considered one of the Grueby firm's greatest achievements. Another example, for instance, was selected as the cover illustration for the catalogue that accompanied the pioneering exhibition on the arts and crafts movement presented by the Princeton University Art Museum in 1972. The original architectural setting of this particular tile is not known. Its flat, stylized rendering of a dense woodland scene, composed of discrete patches of seven colored glazes, recalls the process of abstraction inherent to mosaics, stained glass, and color woodblock prints. Yet the pooling and crackling of the creamy, earth-toned glazes give the tile a richly textured surface all its own. In painterly fashion, the glazes vary from thick to thin, providing subtle tonal modulation within the design elements, as seen particularly in the greens. The fortuitous crackling and segmentation of the glazes—which relied to some extent on the vagaries of the firing process—beautifully simulate the texture of bark and foliage in this example. Perhaps more than any of Grueby's pictorial tiles, it conveys the sophisticated design, skilled craftsmanship, and deep reverence for nature associated with the best of the American arts and crafts movement.

BJM

Clark, Robert Judson. *The Arts and Crafts Movement in America, 1876–1916*. Princeton, NJ: Princeton University Press, 1972.

Kaplan, Wendy. *"The Art That Is Life": The Arts and Crafts Movement in America, 1875–1920*. Boston: Museum of Fine Arts, Boston, 1987.

Montgomery, Susan J. *The Ceramics of William H. Grueby: The Spirit of the New Idea in Artistic Handicraft*. Lambertville, NJ: *Arts and Crafts Quarterly* Press, 1993.

Montgomery, Susan J., with an essay by William P. Curry. *Grueby Pottery, A New England Arts and Crafts Venture: The William Curry Collection*. Hanover, NH: Hood Museum of Art, Dartmouth College, 1994.

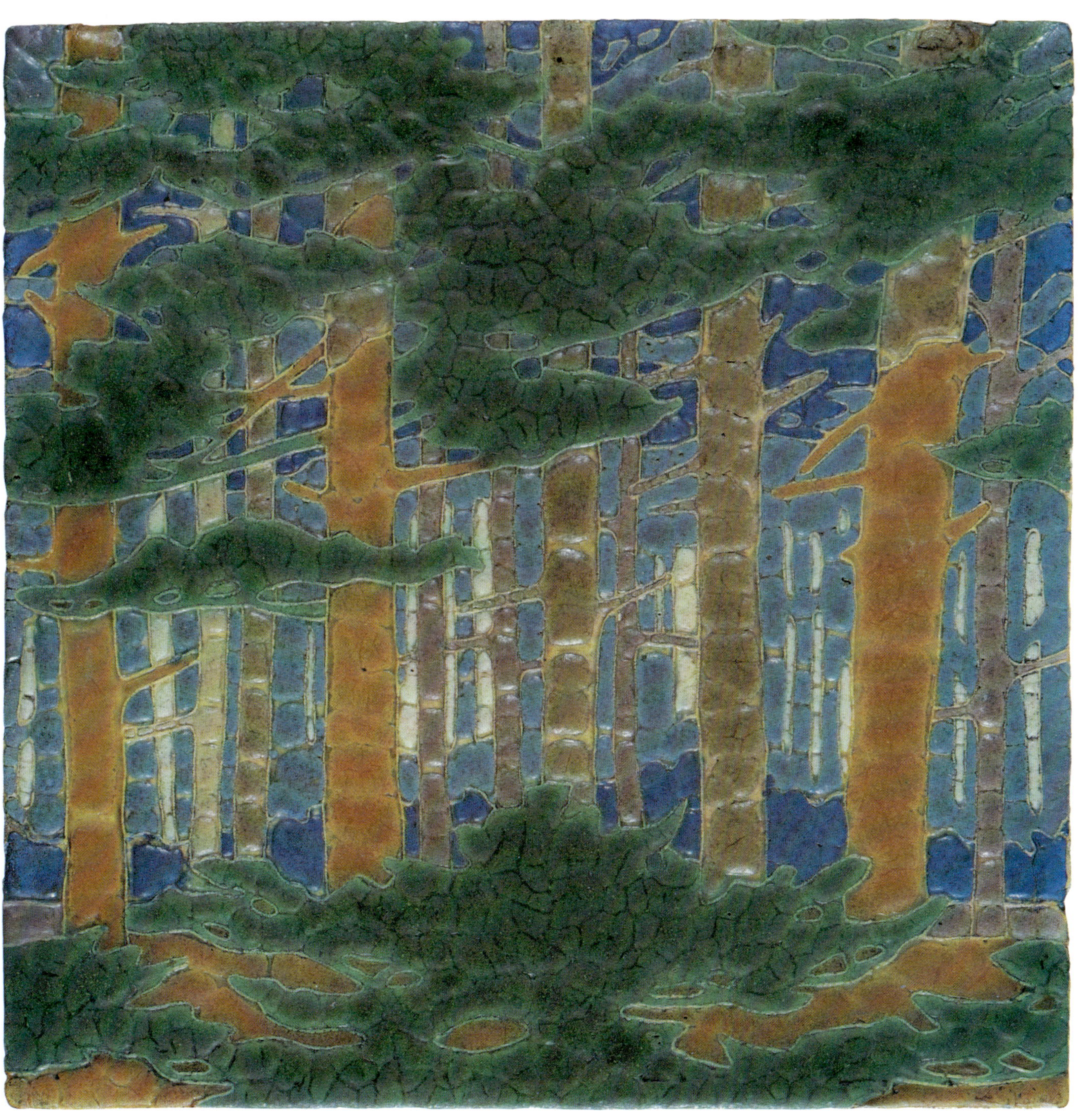

16 **LEWIS WICKES HINE**

American, 1874–1940

A Driver in a Coal Mine, W. Va

Photographed Sept. 1908,
printed ca. 1940
Gelatin silver print
14 x 11 in.

Gift of Franklin Davidson M.D.,
Class of 1955

Lewis Hine was a self-taught photographer who believed strongly in the photograph's potential to convey a truth more clearly than words. From 1906 to 1918, Hine worked for the National Child Labor Committee (NCLC), traveling throughout the United States and photographing child workers in mills, fields, canneries, factories, and mines. As one of the first documentary photographers, he was inventing an aesthetic that could both touch viewers' emotions and persuade them to action. His photographs were used by the NCLC in exhibitions, published pamphlets, periodicals, and as lantern slides by lecturers working to promote legislation that would regulate child labor.

Hine's own caption for this photograph described the boy: "Young Driver in Mine. Has been driving one year. 7 A.M. to 5:30 P.M. daily in Brown Mine. Brown, W. Va." This boy's job would have been to transport coal out of the mines in muledrawn carts throughout the day. The image is a good example of the matter-of-fact approach that Hine brought to his subjects. There is a sense of respect for this boy as a complete individual, while at the same time the grimy details of his working life are captured. His bright eyes shine out of a blackened face, and the looseness of his shirt and overalls emphasizes his youthfulness. Most of Hine's subjects had probably never had their picture taken, and so they do not smile self-consciously but rather stare into the lens with a seriousness that calls attention to their lost innocence. Hine's photographs helped to make child labor a public issue, although it was not until 1938, as part of the Fair Labor Standards Act, that a law was passed to limit the practice.

MWL

Curtis, Verna Posever. *Photography and Reform: Lewis Hine and the National Child Labor Committee*. Milwaukee: Milwaukee Art Museum, 1984.

Goldberg, Vicki. *Lewis W. Hine: Children at Work*. Munich: Prestel, 1999.

Rosenblum, N., W. Rosenblum, and A. Trachtenberg. *America and Lewis Hine: Photographs, 1904–1940*. New York: Aperture, 1977.

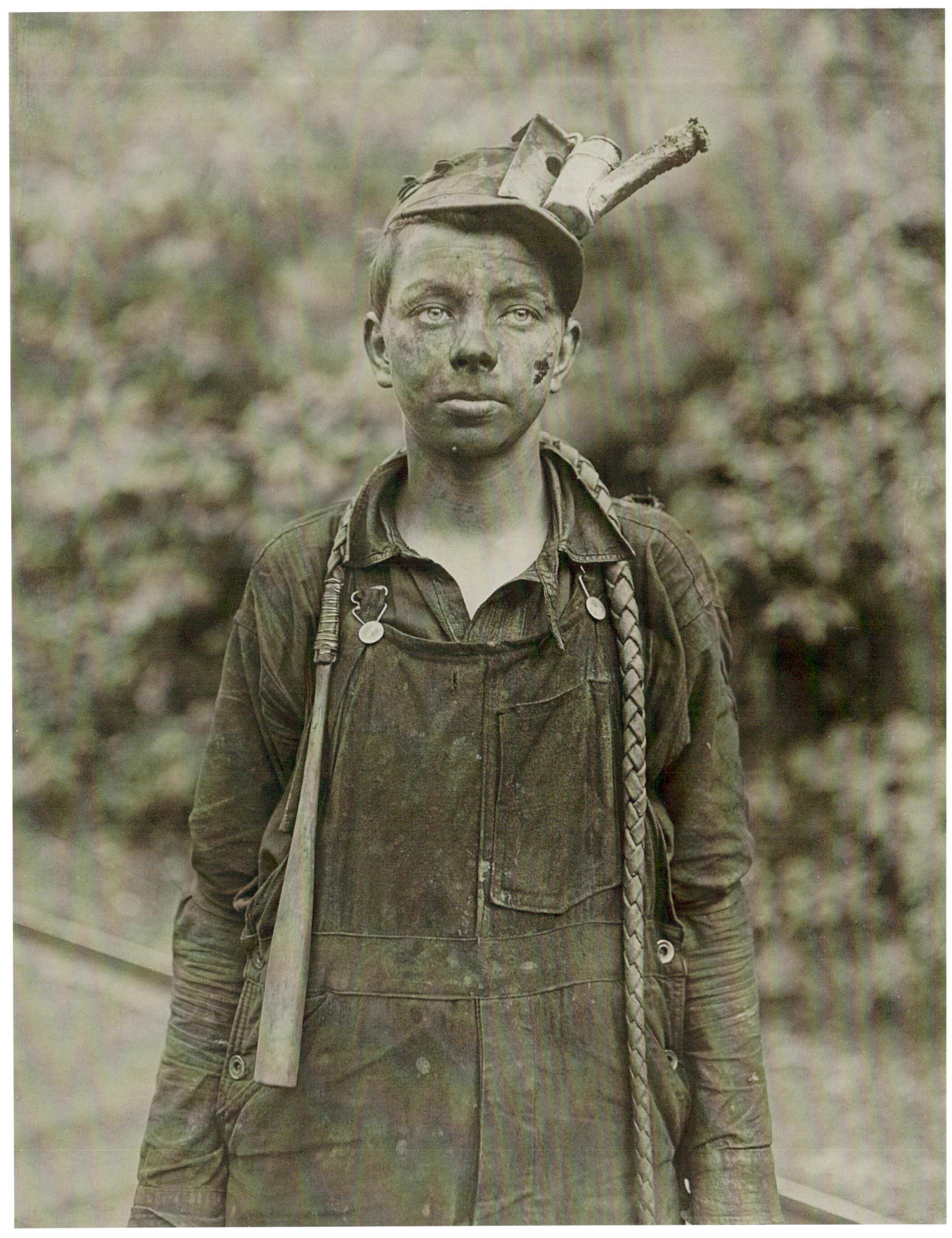

17 **ALEXANDER ARCHIPENKO**

Ukrainian, active in France and the United States, 1887–1964

White Torso

1916, cast around 1930 at the Kunst Foundry, New York
Polished bronze
H: 18 in.

Gift of Harry T. Lewis Jr., Class of 1955, Tuck 1956, DP

Alexander Archipenko was an artist, working mainly in sculpture, who was endlessly striving for innovation and creative invention in his work. Extremely ambitious and independent, he was forced to leave the School of Art in Kiev in 1905 after three years of study because he criticized the academic approach of his teachers. Later, in Paris, following only two weeks of instruction at the École des Beaux-Arts, he turned instead to the collections of the Musée du Louvre for his education. Although he always resisted being defined by any specific movements, Archipenko's early work shows clear influences from the sculpture of Henri Matisse and Constantin Brancusi as well as the ideas and aesthetics of cubism.

Archipenko produced *White Torso* in 1916, while residing in a villa at Cimiez, a suburb of Nice, where he remained throughout World War I. Marble, bronze, and plaster versions of this sculpture exist. The graceful nude form was a central focus of Archipenko's work throughout his artistic development. He wrote, "If muscles or bones interfere with the line, I eliminate them in order to obtain simplicity, purity, and the expression of stylistic line and form" (quoted in Wasserman and Cuno 1980: 62). In this quest for purity, he was certainly inspired by Brancusi, who was one of the first artists to represent the body as a simple arrangement of abstract volumes. Archipenko used polished metal that reflects the light to insist on the qualities of the object's surface and its interaction with the surrounding space. After he immigrated to the United States in 1923, several early casts of the sculpture were produced with different finishes by the Kunst Foundry in New York. In 1929, Archipenko included a version of this work in a Saks Fifth Avenue window display that he designed, which featured a machined metal backdrop (see photograph in Karshan 1969: 73). He angled an armless, headless mannequin draped in a sleek, sleeveless dress toward *White Torso*, perhaps prompting viewers to make comparisons between his streamlined form and the fashionable modern woman. Clearly, the simplicity of design so central to Archipenko's art easily found a place within the commercial and decorative aesthetics of the 1920s and 1930s.

MWL

Archipenko, Alexander. *Archipenko: Fifty Creative Years*. New York: Tekhne, 1960.

Karshan, Donald H., ed. *Archipenko: International Visionary*. Washington, DC: Smithsonian Institution Press, 1969.

Michaelsen, Katherine Jánszky. *Archipenko: A Study of the Early Works, 1908–1920*. New York: Garland Publishing, 1977.

Wasserman, Jeanne L., with contributions by James B. Cuno. *Three American Sculptors and the Female Nude: Lachaise, Nadelman, Archipenko*. Cambridge, MA: Fogg Art Museum, 1980.

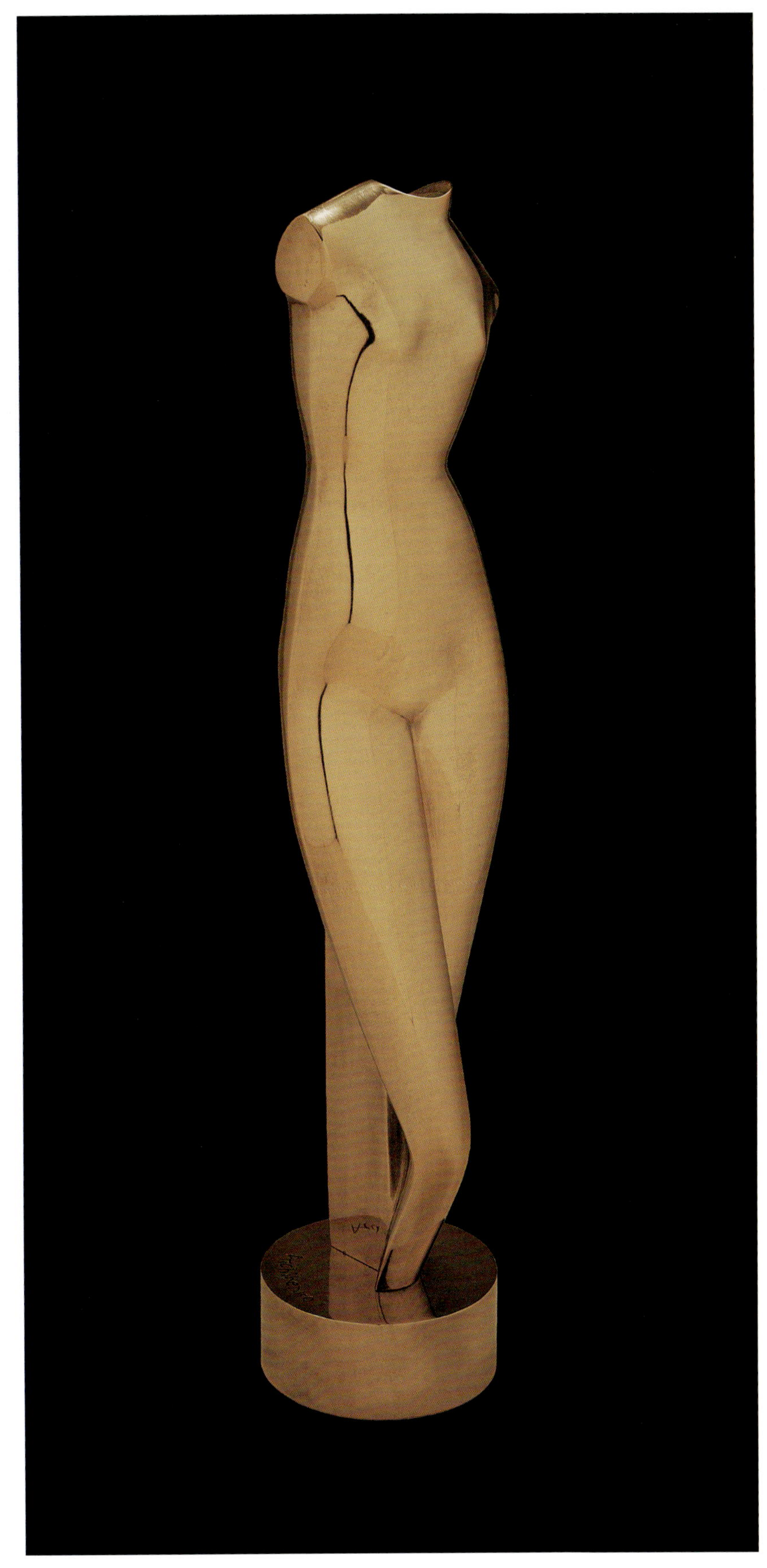

18 GEORGE BELLOWS

American, 1882–1925

Village Massacre

1918
Lithograph
17¾ x 29⅝ in.

Promised gift of Robert Dance, Class of 1977

George Bellows is perhaps best known for his paintings of boxers, in which blood and sweat fly from the glorified bodies of trained fighters. However, an important part of his oeuvre focuses on a very different sort of violence—that directed toward civilians during war. Bellows first arrived in New York City to pursue painting under the tutelage of Robert Henri in 1904, and he was initially associated with the Ashcan school. It was not until 1916 that he became committed to lithography as an expressive medium, employing it as he sought to communicate the horrors and inhumanity of the international conflict that defined his generation—World War I.

In 1918, Bellows produced his *War Series*. While scholars disagree on exactly which works should be included in this grouping, *Village Massacre* (also known as *Massacre at Dinant*) was definitely part of the 1919 exhibition of Bellows's lithographs at the Albert Rollier Art Gallery in Chicago titled *War, Subjects Founded on the Bryce Report*. The Bryce Report was an account of the German invasion of Belgium in August 1915, based on eyewitnesses, that was published in abridged form in the *New York Times* on May 13, 1915. Bellows was profoundly affected by it and based *Village Massacre* directly on its descriptions of the actions of German soldiers in the town of Dinant. He also transposed the composition into paint in the same year. In the print, men, women, and children lie dead, or wail and scream in the face of their imminent fate. The presence of the German soldiers is indicated only by the bayonets that poke into view at the far left, from which a nun recoils.

MWL

George Bellows and the War Series of 1918. New York: Hirschl & Adler Galleries, 1983.

George Wesley Bellows: Paintings, Drawings, and Prints. Columbus, Ohio: Columbus Museum of Art, 1979.

Mason, Lauris, assisted by Joan Ludman. *The Lithographs of George Bellows: A Catalogue Raisonné*. New York: KTO Press, 1977.

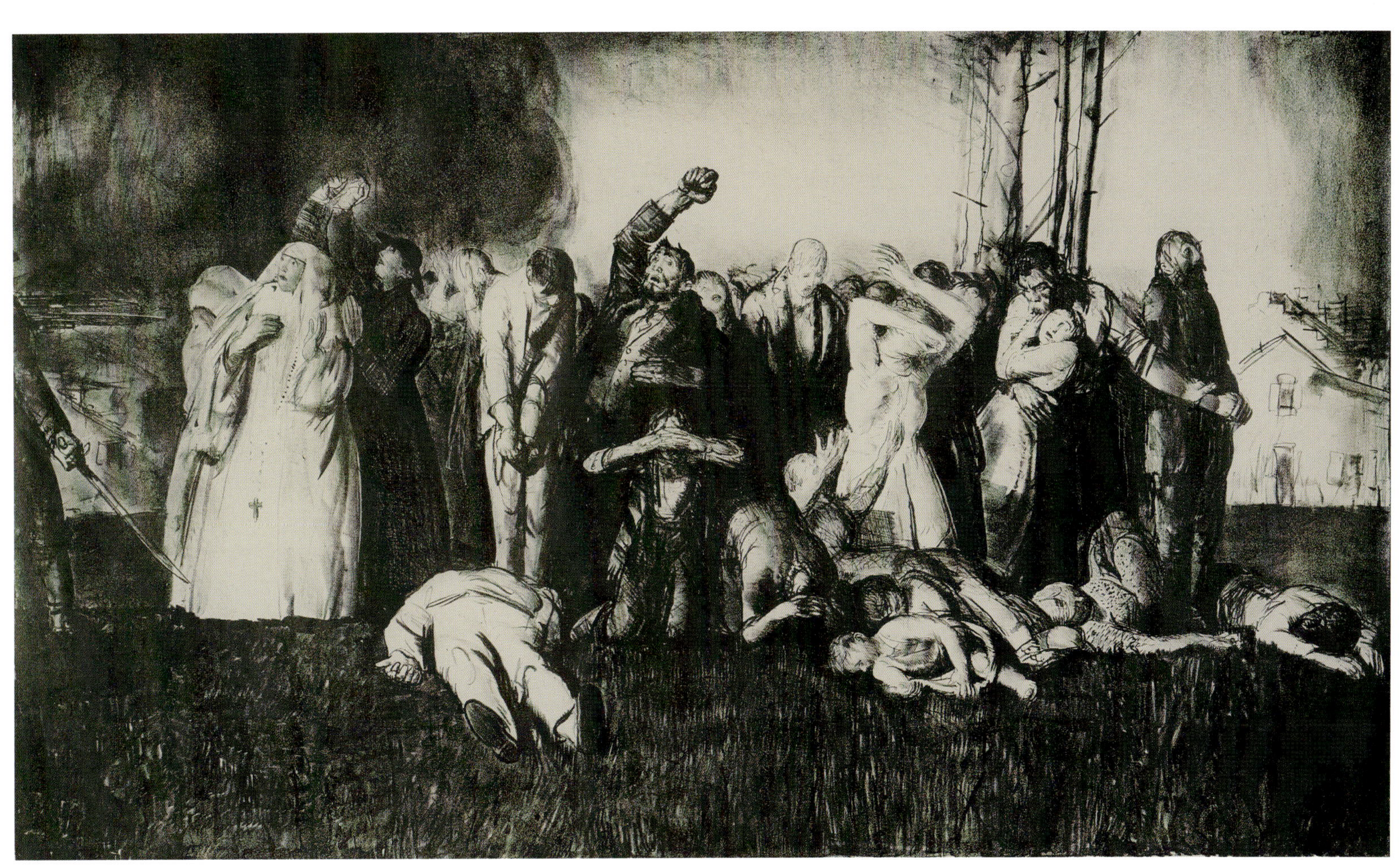

19 **JOHN FOLINSBEE**

American, 1892–1972

Village in Winter

ca. 1918
Oil on canvas
32¼ x 31 in. (sight)

Promised gift of Charles Hood, Class of 1951

Like several of the impressionist landscape painters who worked in the vicinity of New Hope, Pennsylvania, in the early twentieth century, John (Jack) Folinsbee painted rustic, picturesque scenery, often captured in winter. He settled in the region in 1916 at the suggestion of his early mentor, the tonalist landscape painter Birge Harrison. One of several art colonies then flourishing in the Northeast, New Hope attracted artists who enjoyed the camaraderie and painting *plein air* subjects redolent of a bygone era. There Folinsbee joined and was influenced by the slightly older and more established figures associated with Pennsylvania impressionism, including Edward Redfield, Robert Spencer (Harrison's nephew-in-law), and Daniel Garber.

Village in Winter is a prime example of Folinsbee's mature style, for which he received favorable recognition at national exhibitions. The composition reveals his distinctive paint facture, in which parallel strokes of pigment create a decorative, tapestry-like effect. The majestic trees silhouetted against the gray sky similarly reveal his eye for pattern and his attention to the two-dimensional surface of the canvas. *Village in Winter* also demonstrates Folinsbee's growing preference for featuring in his landscapes weathered buildings—often mills and factories—that bear a patina of age and human labor. Here, among a cluster of worn outbuildings, a woman beside a full clothesline stoops over her wash. The subdued light and somewhat gritty content owe a debt to Robert Spencer's mill subjects, while the winter setting recalls the work of the colony's best-known painter, Edward Redfield. However, whereas Redfield generally preferred the brilliant lighting effects of snow at midday, Folinsbee sought out overcast conditions in which subdued, restricted tonalities and soft edges prevailed. For many American landscapists active during the first decades of the twentieth century, a blanket of snow afforded a degree of abstraction and modernity to their subjects, while also providing a note of desired lyricism. Folinsbee achieves in this and other winter landscapes of this period a rewarding mix of poetry and tangible substance, surface decoration and deep human sympathy.

BJM

An American Tradition: The Pennsylvania Impressionists. New York: Beacon Hill Fine Art, 1996.

Cook, Peter. *John Folinsbee*. New York: Kubaba Books, 1994.

Folk, Thomas. *The Pennsylvania School of Landscape Painting: An Original American Impressionism*. Allentown, PA: Allentown Art Museum, 1984.

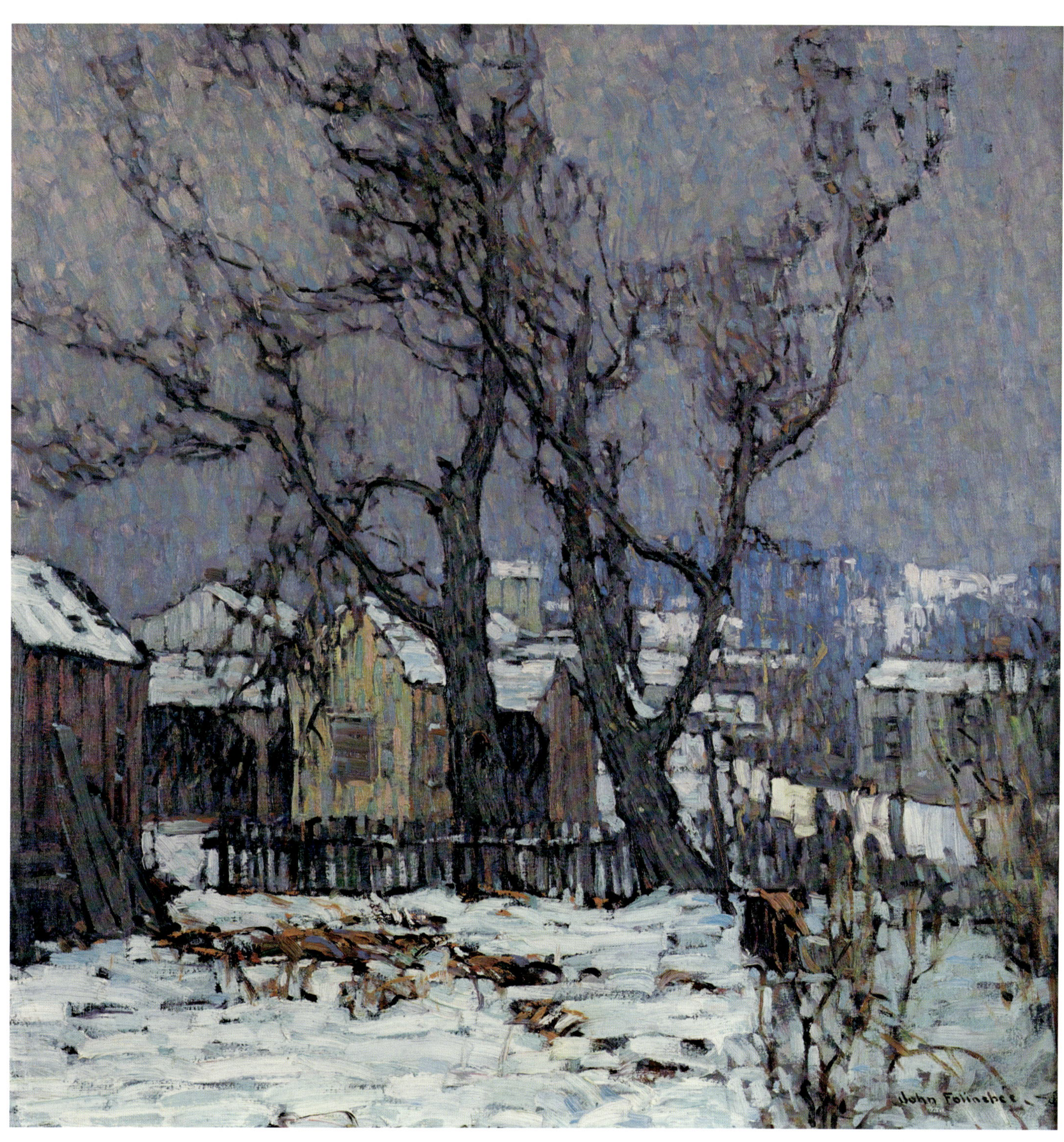
John Folinsbee

20 ROBERT HENRI

American, 1865–1929

Where the Trees Are Dying

1918
Pastel on paper
12½ x 19⅞ in.

Gift of Mr. and Mrs. Jack Huber, Class of 1963

Best known as the dynamic leader of the Ashcan school, a circle of early-twentieth-century urban realist artists, Robert Henri also produced important landscapes and marine scenes, particularly during summer sojourns along the Maine coast. This pastel was created during his productive 1918 visit to Maine's rugged and picturesque Monhegan Island. Henri first discovered Monhegan in 1903 and, like many artists, was taken with the mix of pounding surf, soaring cliffs, and secluded woodlands. He extolled the island's artistic virtues in a letter to his parents: "It is a wonderful place to paint—so much in so small a place one can hardly believe it." He returned in 1911 and again in 1918. During this final visit, he sketched a series of bold, almost abstract, pastels set within the island's dense Cathedral Woods.

The closely cropped, horizontal format of *Where the Trees Are Dying* flattens out the picture plane and accentuates the rhythmic groupings of barren tree trunks, struck with flickering light. Rather than the delicate pastel tints generally associated with the medium, Henri relied primarily on deep earth tones that vividly set off the silvery trunks and contribute to the introspective mood. As noted by the work's elegiac title, the trees—one of which has partially fallen—bear few signs of life. Patches of bright green undergrowth, however, enliven the palette and offer the promise of renewal. In his book, *The Art Spirit*, Henri advised artists to capture "the essence" of a subject, and to combine observation with imagination. In *Where the Trees Are Dying*, he succeeded in creating what he termed an "emotional landscape, . . . like something thought, something remembered."

BJM

Curtis, Jane, and Will and Frank Lieberman. *Monhegan: The Artists' Island*. Camden, ME: Down East Books, 1995.

Nicoll, Jessica F. *The Allure of the Maine Coast: Robert Henri and His Circle, 1903–1918*. Portland, ME: Portland Museum of Art, 1995.

Perlman, Bennard B. *Robert Henri: His Life and Art*. New York: Dover Publications, 1991.

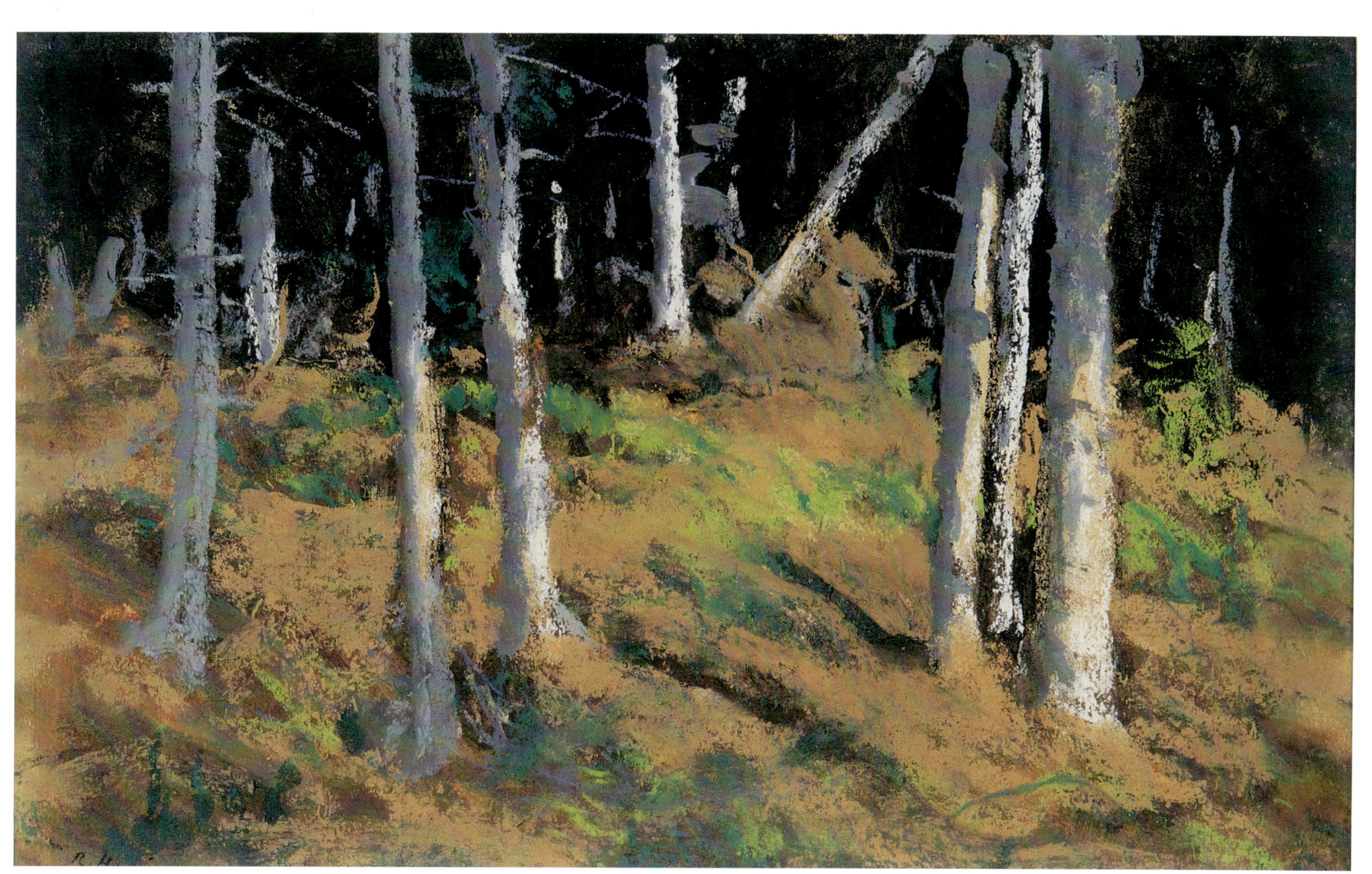

21 **JULIAN MARTINEZ**
American/San Ildefonso Pueblo, 1879–1943

MARIA MONTOYA MARTINEZ
American/San Ildefonso Pueblo, 1887–1980

Jar

ca. 1923–25
Terracotta
H: 8¼ in., Diam: 7½ in.

Gift of Frieda and Prentiss Carnell, Class of 1956

Among the best known black-on-black ware of the American southwest is the San Ildefonso Pueblo pottery, which was developed by Maria Montoya Martinez and her husband, Julian Martinez. Blackened ware was most likely introduced to this part of what is now New Mexico around the year 1000 from what is now Mexico. Some pueblo potters continued to make this blackened ware until the twelfth century, when its production began to lapse. Beginning in the sixteenth century, the costly and labor-intensive blackened ware was further threatened by inexpensive Spanish tin and Anglo enamelware. In 1908 and 1909, Dr. Edgar Lee Hewett, director of the Museum of New Mexico, led excavations of a Pueblo site near San Ildefonso Pueblo, where ancient blackened ware and polychromatic ware were rediscovered. Hewett asked Martinez, already an exemplary Pueblo potter from San Ildefonso Pueblo, to replicate the pottery samples for the museum.

Martinez's involvement in Hewitt's project prompted her and her husband, who painted the designs on the pottery samples after Maria shaped them, to begin an artistic collaboration that revived the thousand-year-old tradition of blackened ware while adapting it to modern tastes. Although other pueblos, such as Santa Clara, had been producing blackened ware before Hewitt's excavations, Maria and Julian Martinez invented a technique that would allow for some areas of the pottery to have a matte finish and others to be a high-luster jet black. Experimenting with this technique between 1918 and 1919, they finally developed the now-famous black-on-black pottery style that has influenced generations of Pueblo artists with carved and matte decorations on monochromatic, polychromatic, and black-on-black pottery.

Over the course of her life, Martinez signed her pottery in several ways. Her early pottery pieces, dating between 1918 and 1923, were unsigned. Between 1920 and 1925, she signed her works using "Marie" (as in this example), which she was told would be more familiar to the non-Indian public buying her wares. She most likely omitted Julian's name from the signature because pottery was considered women's work. From 1925 until Julian's death in 1943, however, both Maria and Julian signed their pottery with "Marie + Julian," reflecting the collaborative nature of these vessels. Through the years her pieces were also signed as "Poh ve ka," "Marie + Santana," "Maria Poveka," and "Maria/Popovi," reflecting the continued legacy of working with other family members.

BT

Chapman, Kenneth Milton, and Francis H. Harlow. *The Pottery of San Ildefonso Pueblo*. Albuquerque: School of American Research and the University of New Mexico Press, 1970.

Peaster, Lillian. *Pueblo Pottery Families: Acoma, Cochiti, Hopi, Isleta, Jemez, Laguna, Nambe, Picuris, Pojoaque, San Ildefonso, San Juan, Santa Clara, Santo Domingo, Taos, Tesuque, Zia, Zuni*. Atglen, PA: Schiffer Publishing, 1997.

Spivey, Richard L. *Maria*. Flagstaff, AZ: Northland Press, 1979.

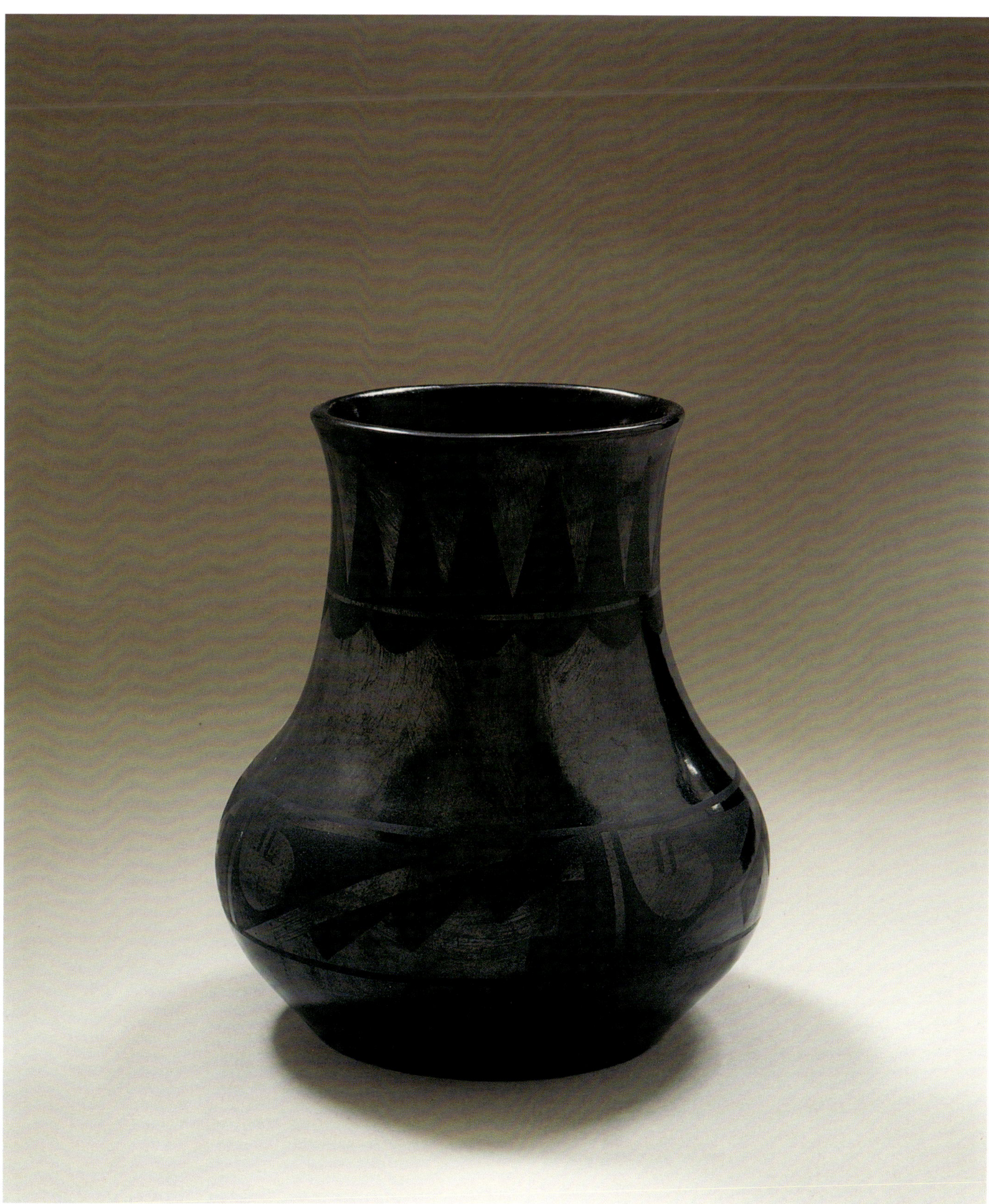

22 **GUSTAVE BAUMANN**

American, 1881–1971

Singing Trees

1928

Color woodcut

12¾ x 12¾ in.

Promised gift of Charles Hood, Class of 1951

Gustave Baumann was a German immigrant to the United States who ultimately found inspiration and contentment in Santa Fe, New Mexico, where he settled in 1918. There he produced the art that has come to define his oeuvre—woodcut prints of the southwestern landscape that, in their strong color palette, evoke the heat and intensity of this region's blazing sun. Baumann was devoted to his art as a specialized craft and, unlike some printmakers, insisted on controlling the entire process, from the design, to the grinding and mixing of dry pigments for the inks, to the mechanical operation of the press. Baumann believed strongly in creating art that would be accessible for everyone. Each of his color prints was an original work, the product of five or six blocks carved directly by him, yet they were affordable for middle-class customers to display in their homes.

Singing Trees was produced following a 1926 trip by Baumann that took him along the coast of California from Laguna to San Francisco Bay. The lush green leaves of these trees suggests that their source of inspiration can be found in these travels rather than the more barren landscape of the Santa Fe region. Baumann crops the trees and brings them close to the picture plane, so that the linear, decorative qualities of the branches and leaves become the work's focus, rather than an illusionistic representation of space. In a practice that was not common among American printmakers at the time, he uses gold leaf to create a glowing background that is reminiscent of medieval Italian painting. Baumann's stamped seal can be found at the bottom right of the sheet—this stylized hand over the heart was based on a Native American design and symbolizes the artist's pledge to his art and his audience.

MWL

Acton, David. *Hand of a Craftsman: The Woodcut Technique of Gustave Baumann.* Santa Fe: Museum of New Mexico Press, 1996.

Krause, Martin F., Madeline Carol Yurtseven, and David Acton. *Gustave Baumann: Nearer to Art.* Santa Fe: Museum of New Mexico Press, 1993.

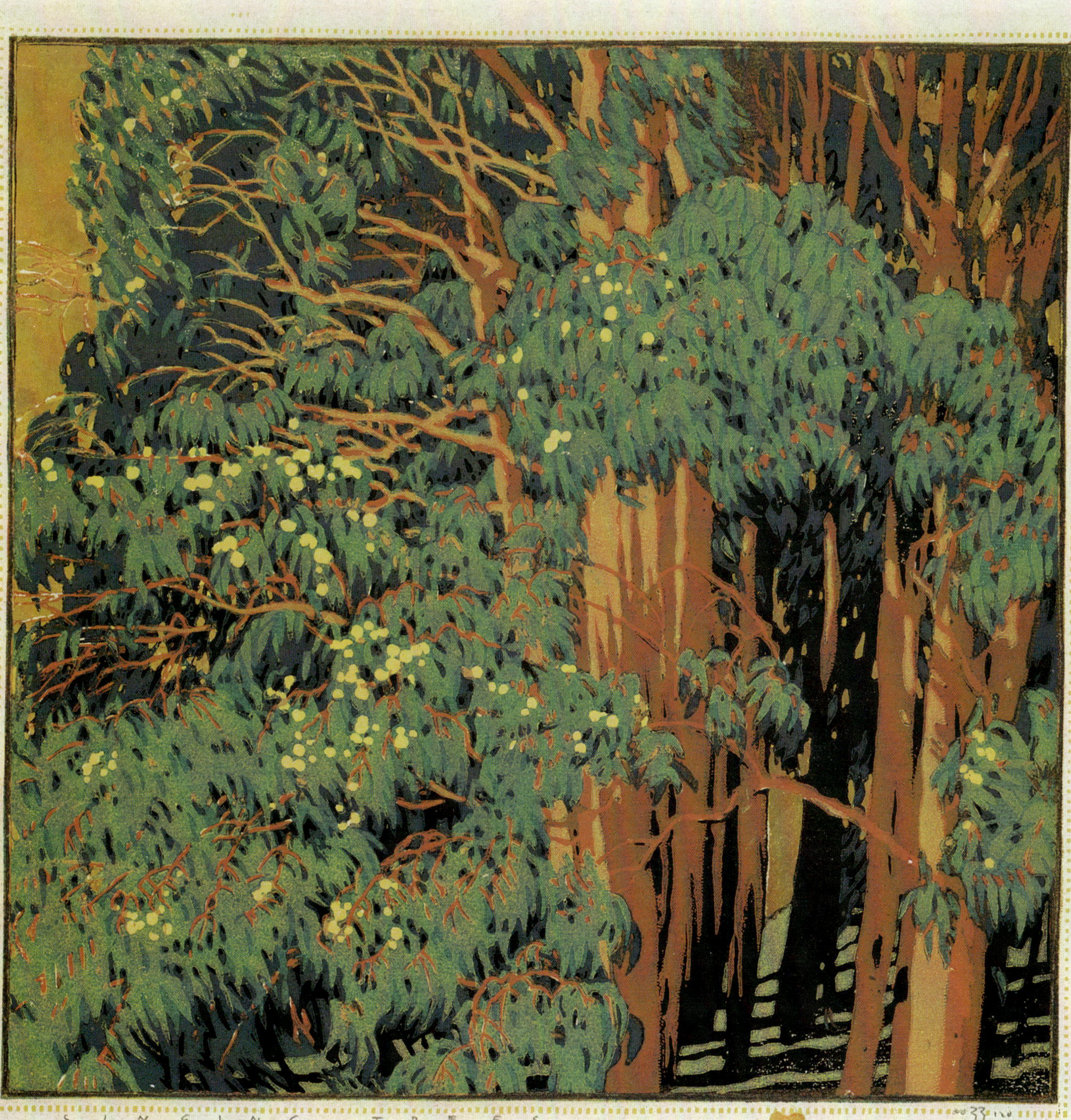
S I N G I N G T R E E S
Gustave Baumann

23 **PAUL SAMPLE**

American, 1896–1974

Speech Near Brewery

1932

Oil on canvas

36 x 40 in.

Promised gift of Charles Hood, Class of 1951

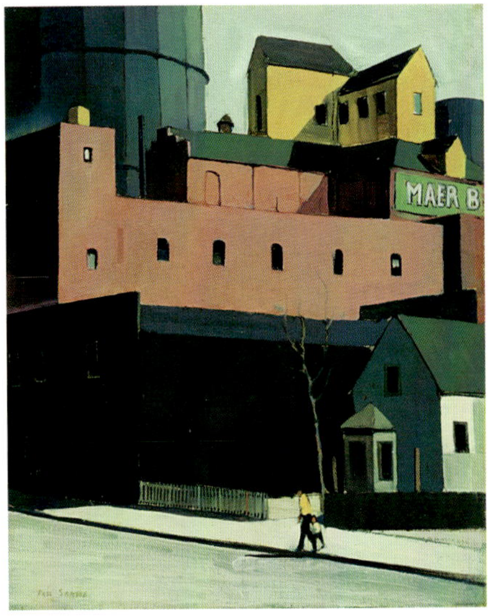

Paul Sample, *Maer Brewery*, 1932.
Oil on canvas, 20⅛ x 16⅛ in. Gift of the artist, Class of 1920; P.983.34.193

Paul Sample, Class of 1920, is arguably the best-known painter to have attended Dartmouth College. He first determined to become an artist in 1923 while recuperating from tuberculosis in a sanitarium in Saranac Lake, New York. There he received informal instruction and important encouragement from the painter Jonas Lie, whose wife was also being treated. Once recovered, Sample took up studies at the Otis Art Institute in Los Angeles in 1925. By the mid-1930s he had become chairman of the art department at the University of Southern California; he was exhibiting his paintings nationally; and he was participating in a lively circle of California painters and watercolorists. He returned to Dartmouth in 1938 as artist-in-residence, a position he held until his retirement in 1962. He is known especially for his regionalist images of New England's bucolic landscape and colorful smalltown life.

Speech Near Brewery is a preeminent example of Sample's earlier California period, during which he often explored social realist themes in semiabstracted urban settings. This ambitious painting, which he exhibited at the Corcoran Gallery of Art in 1933, is based on a smaller oil study of the brewery in the collection of the Hood Museum of Art (see the comparative image included here). In the final version he expanded the view, inexplicably changed the identification on the building from "Maer B" to "Mana Co Brewery," and animated the desolate industrial image with figures, telephone wires, and a bright yellow automobile. The focal point is a propagandist delivering an impassioned speech on a soapbox to a small gathering crowd of male, possibly unemployed, listeners. The image thereby acknowledges the pressing social concerns and politically charged climate of the depression era—common subjects for artists active in the 1930s. However, the painting's clear warm palette, cheerful, caricature-like figuration, and strong geometric underpinnings are more revealing of Sample's delight with pattern and color and his generalized human interest than his promotion of a burning social agenda.

BJM

Haletsky, John. *Paul Sample, Ivy League Regionalist*. Miami: Lowe Art Museum, University of Miami, 1984.

McGrath, Robert L., with an extended chronology by Paula F. Glick. *Paul Sample: Painter of the American Scene*. Hanover, NH: Hood Museum of Art, Dartmouth College, distributed by University Press of New England, 1988.

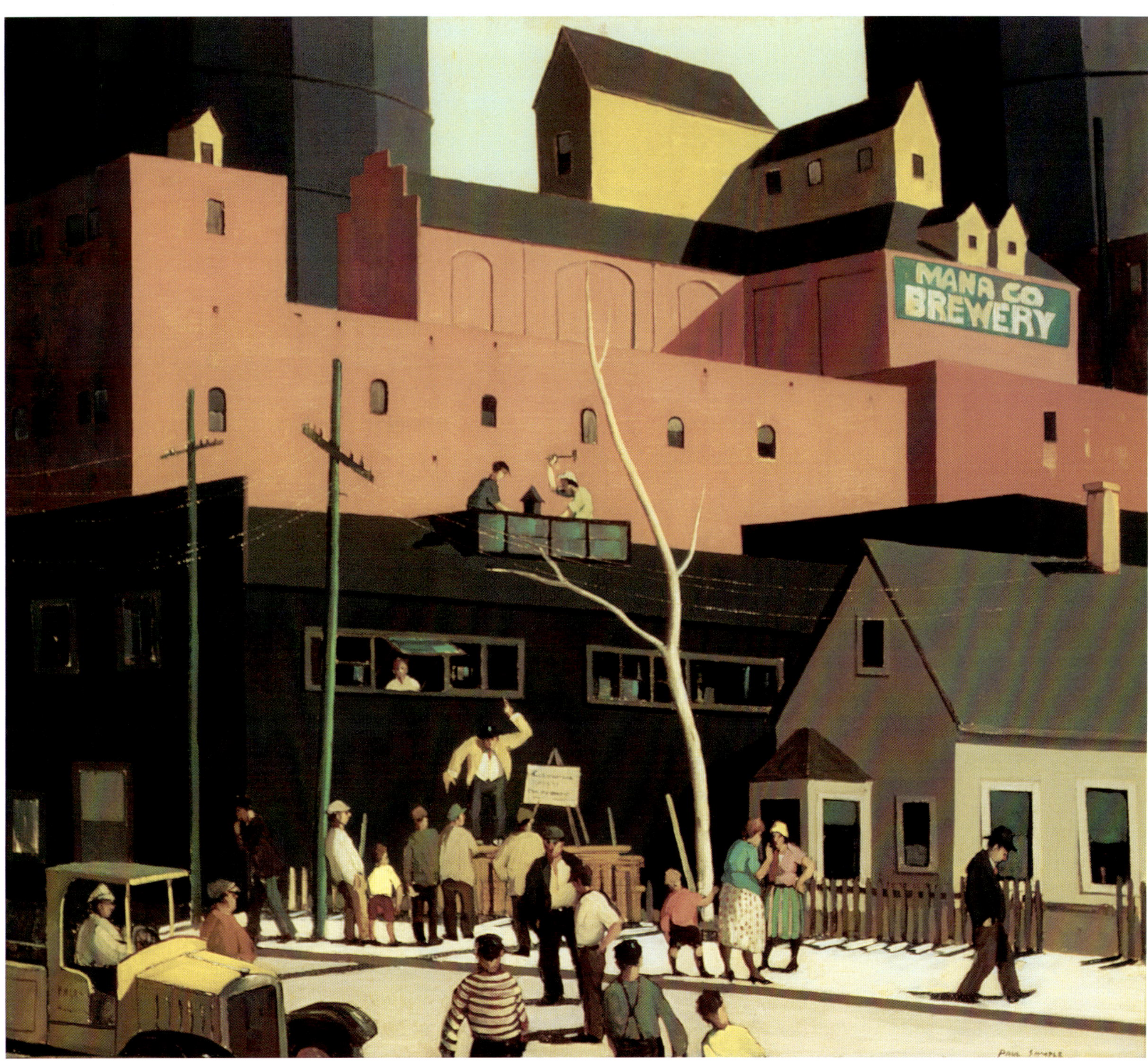
MANA CO
BREWERY

24 RUFINO TAMAYO

Mexican, 1899–1991

Portrait of Rosalind Richards

1948
Oil, charcoal, and pastel on gessoed masonite
48 x 36 in.

Gift of Lois and H. W. Broido Jr., Class of 1951, Tuck 1952, and Eric Richards

Rufino Tamayo came to artistic maturity in Mexico during the postrevolutionary period, when the three great Mexican muralists, Orozco, Rivera, and Sisqueiros, were breaking onto the international art scene. Unlike his slightly older contemporaries, Tamayo showed less interest in expressing didactic themes through art and focused instead on form, color, and aesthetic values, turning to Mexican pre-Columbian art for formal and thematic inspiration. After the first of his many visits to New York, in 1926, Tamayo was greatly impacted by European and American modernism. A highly prolific painter, Tamayo's greatest period of creative maturity began in New York around 1940. During these years, Tamayo's painted forms became increasingly expressionistic, due both to his use of a restricted color palette and to his choice of subject matter (Phillips Collection 1978). During a period that gave rise to abstract expressionism, pop art, and minimalism, Tamayo remained thoroughly devoted to a painterly, controlled approach to the canvas (Genauer 1974). As a result, he explored his expressionistic tendencies through form, texture, and, above all, color.

Portrait of Rosalind Richards embodies the formal language and painterly style of Tamayo's middle years. Rosalind and her husband, Irving Richards, a well-known industrial designer who collaborated with Russell Wright, were friends of Tamayo during the 1940s in New York. In this painting, the figure of Rosalind is reduced to simplified geometric shapes, yet it remains distinctly feminine and articulated. The woman's lyrical attenuation and flattened perspective recall Matisse's portraits of solitary women. Matisse's sensuous and vibrant colors are substituted here for a more somber, glowing palette, and his lightness and dependence upon line are replaced by a darker, more controlled composition. Tamayo's use of a highly muted palette and of a central, static figure pays homage to the figural tradition of pre-Columbian art (Genauer 1974) and typifies Tamayo's own formalist aesthetics and desire to achieve pictorial purity (Paz 1982). As a result, here and elsewhere, the subject matter he has chosen to represent takes a backseat to the interplay of color and light.

VVC

Genauer, Emily. *Rufino Tamayo*. New York: Abrams, 1974.

Paz, Octavio. "Tamayo: Geometry and Transfiguration." In *Rufino Tamayo*, ed. Jacques Lassaigne and Octavio Paz. Barcelona: Ediciones Poligrafa, 1982. 7–21.

Rufino Tamayo: Fifty Years of His Painting. Washington, DC: Phillips Collection, 1978.

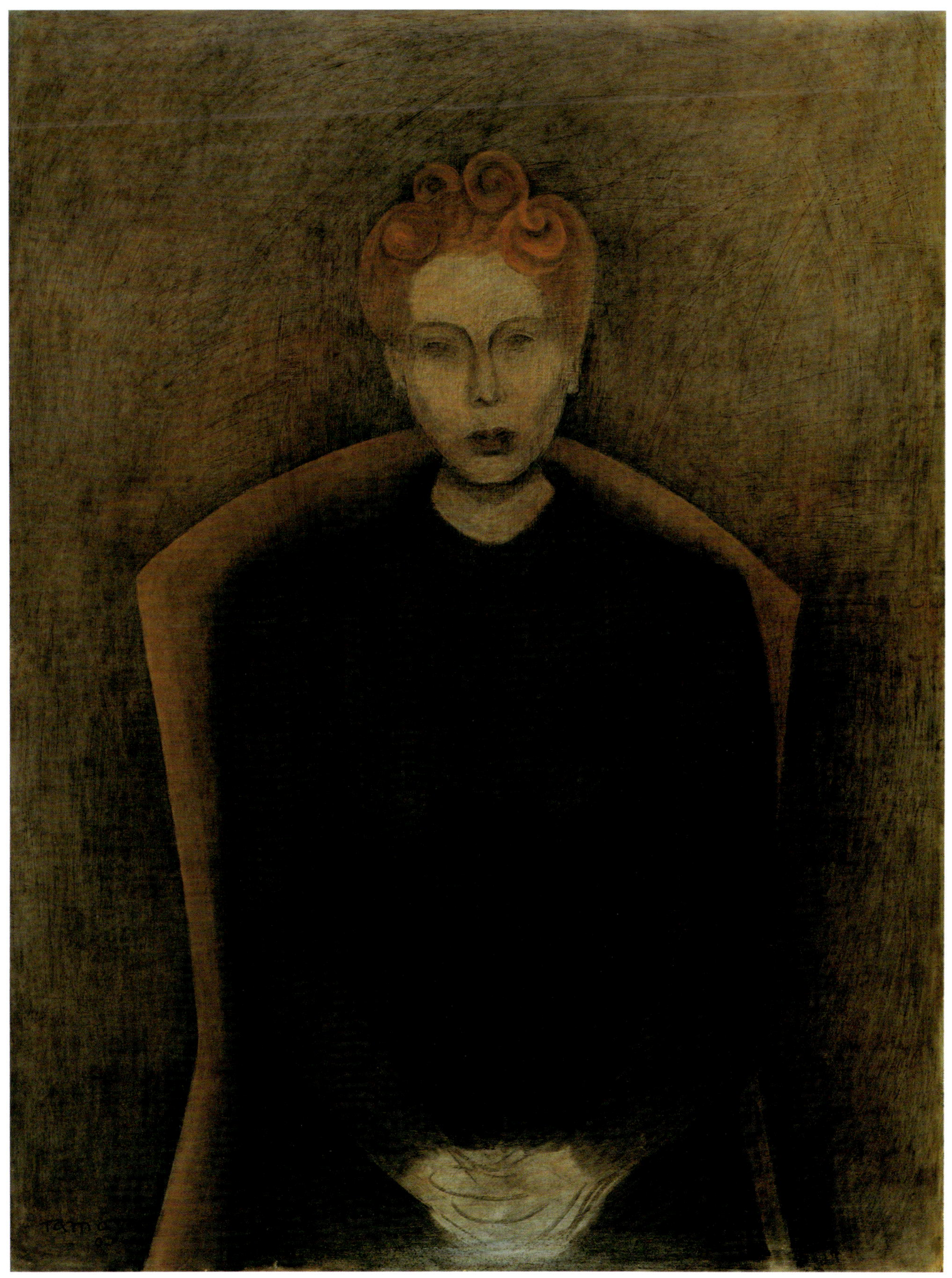

25 **ANDRÉ PIERRE**
Haitian, born 1916

a) Ritual jar *(govi)* for Ezili Freda

Oil paint on fired clay
H: 8¾ in.

b) *Coq Ogoun*

1950s–1966
Oil paint on calabash *(kwi)*
5½ x 12 x 10 in.

26 **SISSON BLANCHARD**
Haitian, 1929–1981

Untitled (Owl)

1960s
Oil paint on masonite
15¾ x 11¾ in.

27 Unknown artist, Haiti

Pakèt Kongo

Before 1966
Mixed media
H: 15¼ in.

Gifts of Micaela and Jack Mendelsohn, Class of 1956

Brown, Karen McCarthy. *Tracing the Spirit: Ethnographic Essays on Haitian Art from the Collection of the Davenport Museum of Art.* Davenport, IA: Davenport Museum of Art, in conjunction with the University of Washington Press, 1995.

Cosentino, Donald, ed. *Sacred Arts of Haitian Vodou.* Los Angeles: UCLA Fowler Museum of Cultural History, 1995.

In 1944, the American watercolorist DeWitt Peters founded the Centre d'Art in Port-au-Prince, Haiti, thereby introducing multiple generations of both self-taught and schooled Haitian painters to the international art world. These artists translated their everyday environment and religious observances onto canvas, cardboard, and a multitude of religious objects devoted to the Afro-Caribbean religion of Vodou. Using bright colors, intricate detail, and playful forms, these Haitian artists reflected the vibrant nature of both secular and sacred life in Haiti through their arts.

Sisson Blanchard, who was born in Trouin, a small village in the mountains of southern Haiti, migrated to Port-au-Prince as a young man; there, the American sculptor Jason Seley encouraged him to paint at the Centre d'Art. Blanchard began painting in 1948 and became one of the first generation of artists to take part in the international rise of Haitian modernist art. Blanchard's paintings focused primarily on secular farming scenes and depictions of birds, usually the owl and the chicken, both of which play an important role in Haiti's Vodou. Blanchard often emphasized the mysterious character of his nocturnal birds with bold outlines and strong contrasting backgrounds.

André Pierre was born in Port-au-Prince, where at an early age he was drawn to Vodou. He became an active practitioner and then a priest of the faith, using art as a means of illustrating the Vodou pantheon of deities. His paintings are characterized by the use of bright, intense colors. In 1949, Pierre was introduced to the Centre d'Art in Port-au-Prince by the filmmaker Maya Deren, who had admired his wall murals in Vodou temples. Before painting on board and canvas, Pierre painted detailed and vibrantly colored representations and emblematic symbols (*vevé*) of the deities (*lwas*) on the inside of hollowed-out calabashes (*kwi*) and decorated earthen vessels (*govi*). While the calabashes contain food offerings in Vodou practices, the ceramic vessels—such as this example, which is emblematic of Ezili Freda, the goddess of love and luxury—are used to capture and contain the spirit essences of deceased members of the Vodou family. These objects, along with the *pakèt kongo*, a spirit-activated healing bundle filled with leaves, herbs, earth, and other ingredients, are reverently placed in the temple to help amplify the healing nature of Vodou.

BT

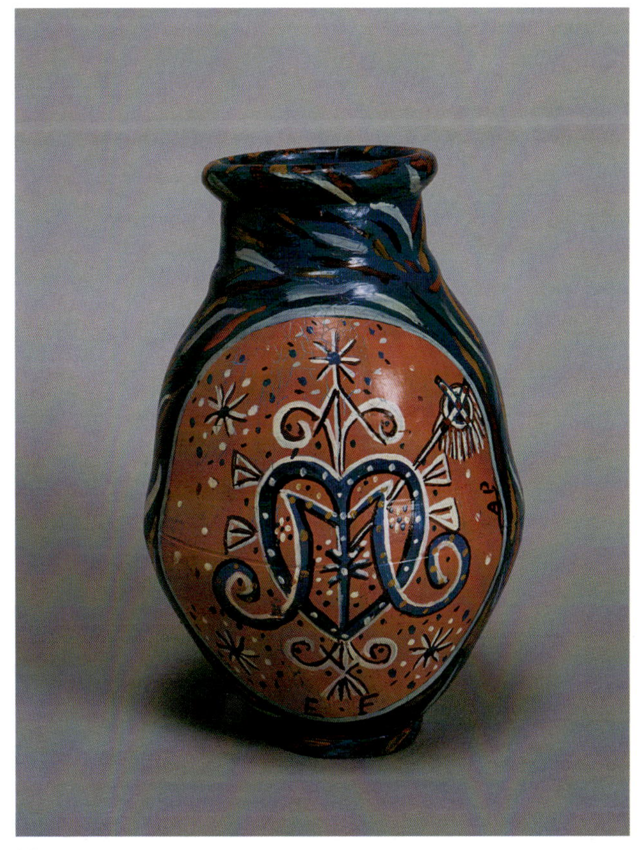

25a

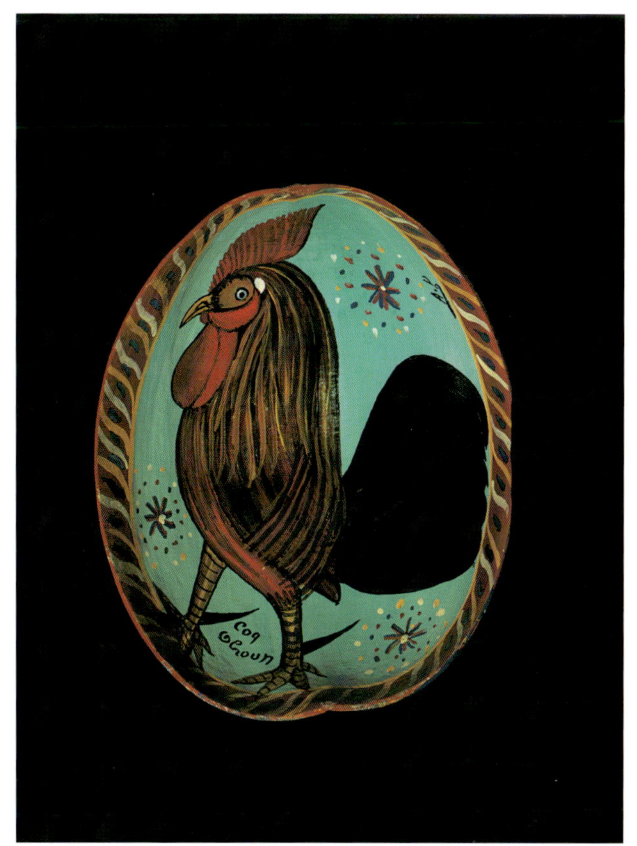

25b

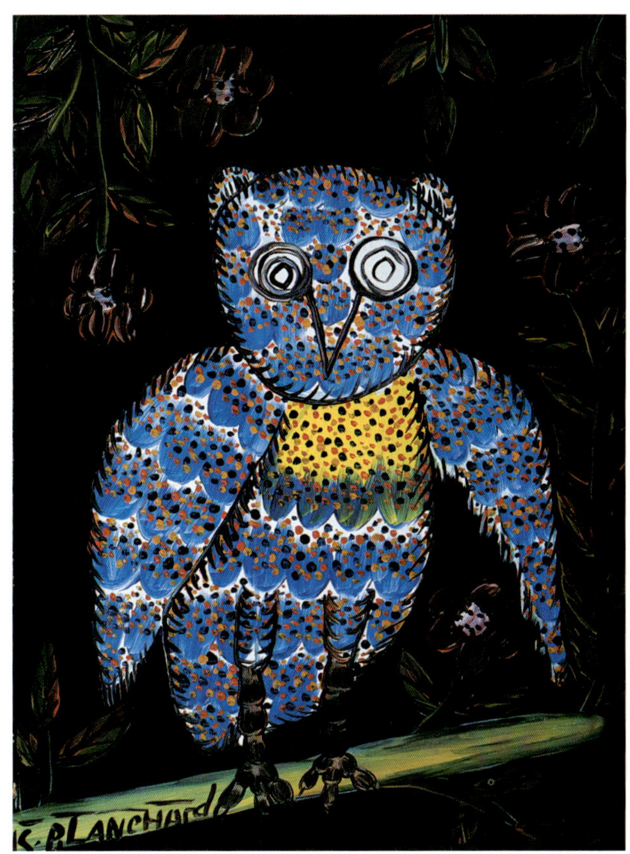

26

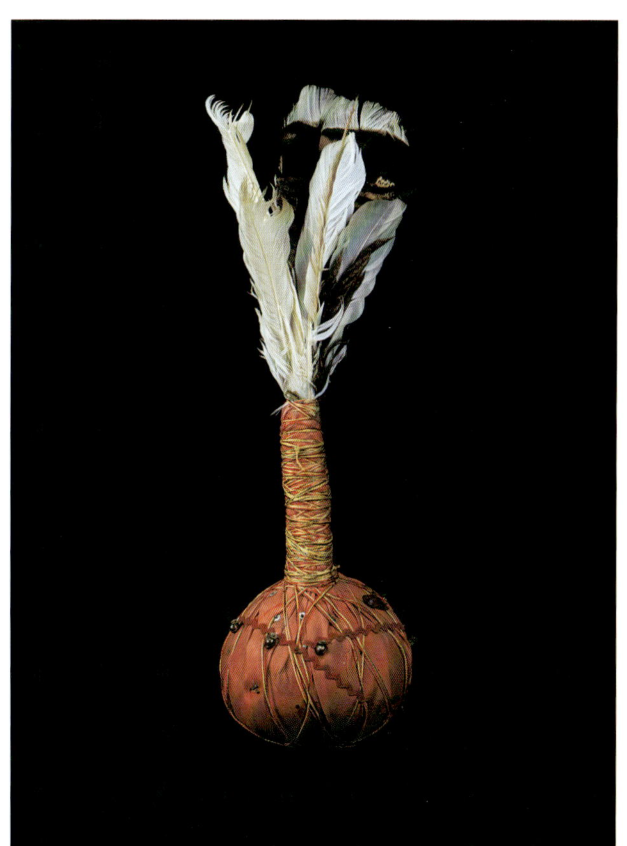

27

28 **VITO ACCONCI**

American, born 1940

Command Performance

Documentation of a performance, January 19, 1974
Photographs and white crayon on paper
Sheet: 20¾ x 20½ in., frame: 21¾ x 21½ in.

Promised gift of Monroe Denton, Class of 1968, in honor of Richard Blum, Class of 1953, and Harriet Warm

Vito Acconci made his mark in the early 1970s with a series of performance works that often applied the scientific method to a series of actions involving his body. His later work does not directly involve his own live performance. A hallmark of his early performance work is its personal edginess, often involving bodily manipulation, fluids, or excretions. In *Conversions* (1971), Acconci burns the hair off his breasts and pulls at them, making them more female in appearance, and in *Trappings* (1971), he sits in a space filled with items from a young girl's bedroom and dresses his penis in doll's clothes. This self-emasculation draws attention to and undermines norms of male identity as defined by accepted sexual and social behavior and practices. In another notorious piece, titled *Seedbed* (1972), he built a floor ramp into a corner of Sonnabend Gallery that had the appearance of a minimalist sculpture. As visitors walked on the sculpture, Acconci, unseen, lay underneath the floorboards of the sculpture and masturbated while audibly voicing his sexual fantasies.

Command Performance, which is documented in the work listed here, was an installation at 112 Greene Street, an alternative art and performance space in New York. He created the piece right after what, in his words, "turned out to be the last live performances I have done; the piece then functioned as a kind of program piece, an announcement of intentions" (Brentano 1981: 56). The work involved a dark room into which the visitor walked. A diagram in the documentation shows the setup: at the foot of a column both a monitor and a video camera face a stool, which is lit by a spotlight and placed against the next column. The image of the stool is transmitted to a monitor in front of a third column. A rug is placed in front of the monitor, where the artist intended visitors to sit. The monitor facing the stool shows Acconci's image, seen from above. He is humming and dreaming of "you who happen to be there." His recorded image speaks to the visitor, with paranoid overtones: "You can show yourself to them, but in the end you'll come back to me, won't you . . . they can see you, you hate them, you keep it inside . . . you can't keep it inside, you turn against them, you're turning against me . . . you have a purpose, you're starting a revolution." These ramblings are accompanied by his insistent humming. This sense of being watched and watching, the disembodied voice and empty stool, were indeed precursors to later works, in which Acconci's voice is a primary element but he himself is no longer present (as the empty stool portends).

KWH

Brentano, Robyn, ed., with Mark Savitt. *112 Workshop/112 Greene Street: History, Artists, and Artworks*. New York: New York University Press, 1981.

Kirshner, J. R. *Vito Acconci: A Retrospective, 1969–1980*. Chicago: Museum of Contemporary Art, 1980.

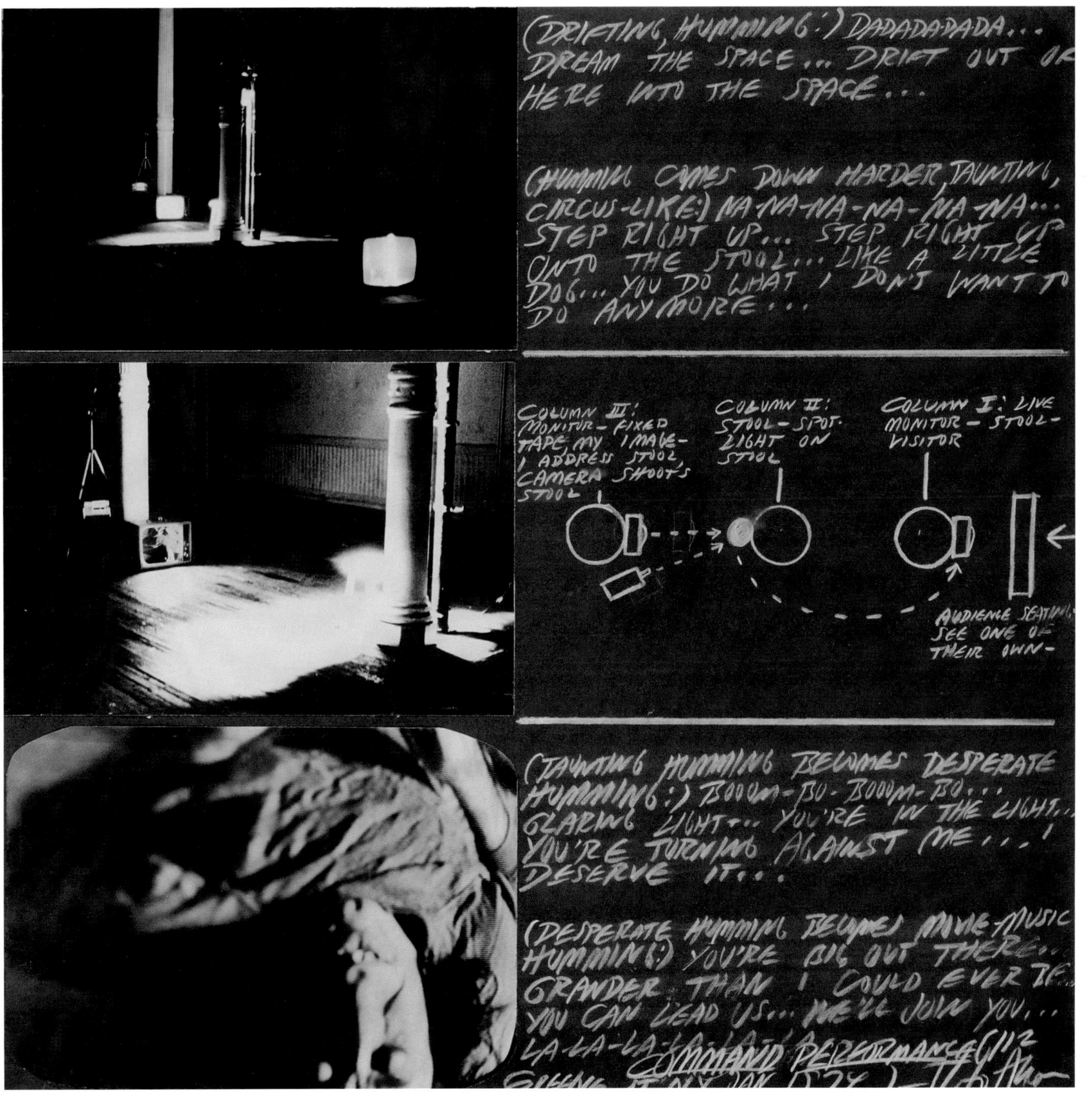
(DRIFTING, HUMMING:) DADADADADA...
DREAM THE SPACE... DRIFT OUT OF
HERE INTO THE SPACE...
(HUMMING COMES DOWN HARDER, TAUNTING,
CIRCUS-LIKE:) NA-NA-NA-NA-NA-NA...
STEP RIGHT UP... STEP RIGHT UP
ONTO THE STOOL... LIKE A LITTLE
DOG... YOU DO WHAT I DON'T WANT TO
DO ANYMORE...
COLUMN III: MONITOR - FIXED TAPE, MY IMAGE - I ADDRESS STOOL CAMERA SHOOTS STOOL
COLUMN II: STOOL - SPOT-LIGHT ON STOOL
COLUMN I: LIVE MONITOR - STOOL - VISITOR
AUDIENCE SEATING - SEE ONE OF THEIR OWN -
(TAUNTING HUMMING BECOMES DESPERATE
HUMMING:) BOOOM-BO-BOOOM-BO...
GLARING LIGHT... YOU'RE IN THE LIGHT...
YOU'RE TURNING AGAINST ME... I
DESERVE IT...
(DESPERATE HUMMING BECOMES MOVIE-MUSIC
HUMMING:) YOU'RE BIG OUT THERE...
GRANDER THAN I COULD EVER BE...
YOU CAN LEAD US... WE'LL JOIN YOU...
LA-LA-LA-LA-LA-LA
COMMAND PERFORMANCE

29 CAROLEE SCHNEEMANN

American, born 1939

American I Ching Apple Pie

Documentation of performance from May 1977
Photographs and typewriting on paper
Sheet: 20½ x 20½ in., frame: 21¼ x 21¼ in.

Promised gift of Monroe Denton, Class of 1968, in honor of Charlet Davenport

Carolee Schneemann was one of the early feminist performance artists and filmmakers, and she worked to redefine the female body and female sexuality against the dominant culture of commercially and socially defined norms. In the era of *Playboy* centerfolds and the sexual revolution of the 1960s and 1970s, Schneemann and other early feminist artists such as Judy Chicago and Sylvia Sleigh sought to emerge from the margins of the art world and work within the new framework for artistic discourse established by women. Many of Schneemann's performances and films from this period involved naked performers and openly embraced evocations of the sexual act, including *Fuses* (1964–67), which caused a small riot among the male members of the audience when it was shown in Cannes in 1968. By 1977, Schneemann had produced some of her most significant performance work, including *Interior Scroll* (1975), in which she stood on a table, painted her nude body with three large strokes of a brush, then performed a series of life model poses, after which she pulled a feminist text in a long scroll from her vagina and read it to the assembled audience. Dan Cameron writes in his essay for a monographic exhibition on her work in 1997, "The transgressive aspect of Schneemann's nudity was a key element in the way these issues transcended sculpture and became political acts, charged by the public spectacle of a woman dictating the terms by which her body could be viewed, and in so doing ensuring that her work would be misconstrued" (Schneemann and Cameron 1997: 11).

In *American I Ching Apple Pie*, Schneemann documents with six photographs a performance from May 1977 in which she took items from a jumble or garage sale, pulled back her hair with a rag, and then sold other donated items as if they were baked goods. Her evocation of the traditional roles of women as organizers of charity events and bakers of items for fairs and church socials places this work at the time when the women's movement had just begun to achieve some its goals for the employment of women in nontraditional careers. In the text that accompanies the photographs, she states, "Go into the kitchen with defient [*sic*] joyful anger. On this scruffy battle ground you can lay down the cookbook forever. You will cease competition with untold legions of sublimated female psyches engaged over the centuries in a pursuit of excellence through flour grease onion turnips." The text also gives loose instructions on how to make an apple pie and alludes to the mystical ancient Chinese text of the I Ching, which became popular in the United States during the 1960s and 1970s as part of a growing fascination with alternative Asian religions. In *Looseleaf* (1964), a related performance work done over a decade earlier at the Judson Dance Theater in New York, an apron-wearing Schneemann sets a table on stage as two men appear from the audience to sit at it. She serves them cake and water, emphasizing the domestic role of women and the expectation that they serve men. Both this performance and *American I Ching Apple Pie* emerge from very time-specific social and political issues about the traditional and limiting domestic role of women.

KWH

Schneemann, Carolee, with Dan Cameron. *Carolee Schneemann: Up to and Including Her Limits.* New York: New Museum of Contemporary Art, 1997.

Schneemann, Carolee, with Bruce McPherson. *More than Meat Joy: Complete Performance Works and Selected Writings.* New Paltz, NY: Documentext, 1979.

CAROLEE SCHNEEMANN

AMERICANA I CHING APPLE PIE

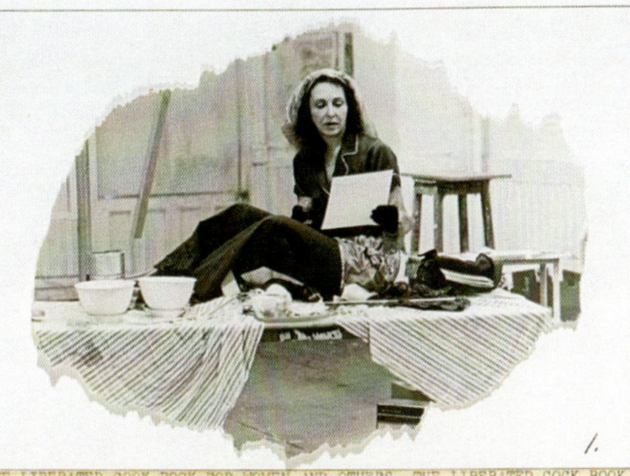

1.

THE LIBERATED COOK BOOK FOR WOMEN AND OTHERS THE LIBERATED COCK BOOK FOR WOMEN AND OTHERS *** AMERICANA I CHING APPLE PIE *** Go into the kitchen with defient joyful anger. On this scruffy battleground you will lay down the cookbook forever. You will cease competition with untold legions of sublimated female psyches engaged over the centuries in a pursuit of excellence through flour grease onion turnips pots blenders collander strainer boilers mincers graters choppers fork whiskers beaters DESIST DESIST STOP STOP NOW! Put on an apron and

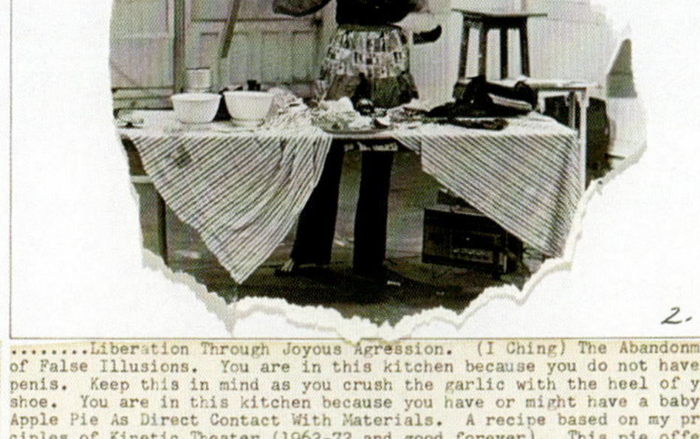

2.

........Liberation Through Joyous Agression. (I Ching) The Abandonment of False Illusions. You are in this kitchen because you do not have a penis. Keep this in mind as you crush the garlic with the heel of your shoe. You are in this kitchen because you have or might have a baby. Apple Pie As Direct Contact With Materials. A recipe based on my principles of Kinetic Theater (1962-72 and good forever). This pie offers self-realization. You will be The Best Woman In The World. AMERICAN AS APPLE PIE. JUST LIKE MUM'S. Remember: the oven is your womb! Let's

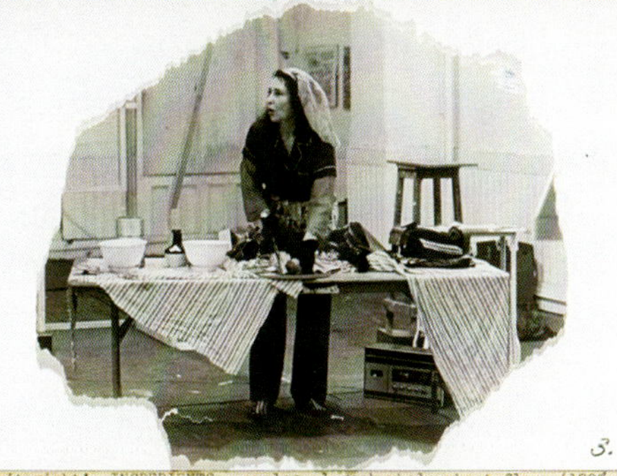

3.

do it right! INGREDIENTS: apples 1 sack whole wheat flour (100% stone ground) barbados sugar egg yolks safflower oil butter honey cinnamon lemon Open flour sack with yr right hand & scoup up 3 handfuls, drop into a bowl. Pinch off a big lump of butter, drop in bowl. Pour in 2 quick turns of oil. Add small pile brown sugar. Use both hands to scrunch it all up in yr finger tips to nice crumby mass -- soft. Sprinkle a few drops of cold water on top, mix again. Now it is sticky & ready to be patted into a baking dish.....or two. Might as

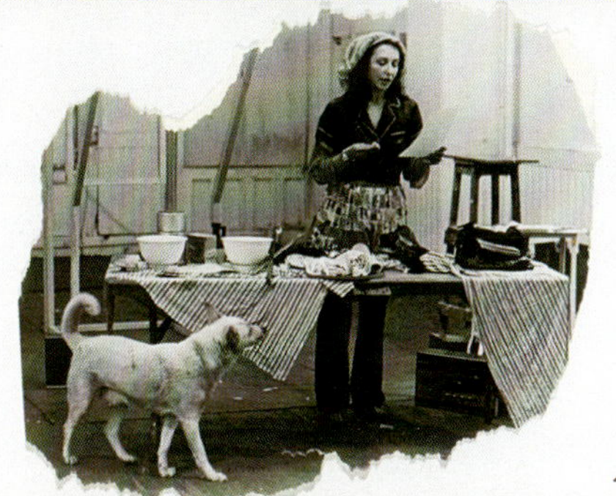

4.

well make two pies. Slide hunk of butter all over baking dishes. Wash apples (don't peel if organically grown). Pat pastry all over the dish. Use small lumps which you press flat until they all mesh & cover dish. Now you can make those cute finger indentations along the top! Sprinkle with cinnamon, bits of sugar, butter bits, lemon juice, drips of honey. If you have some yogurt or sour cream, take yr fingers & smear it over apple tops.....Have Faith! Note: if any ingredients fall on the floor just pick them up & put them where they should have gone. My father

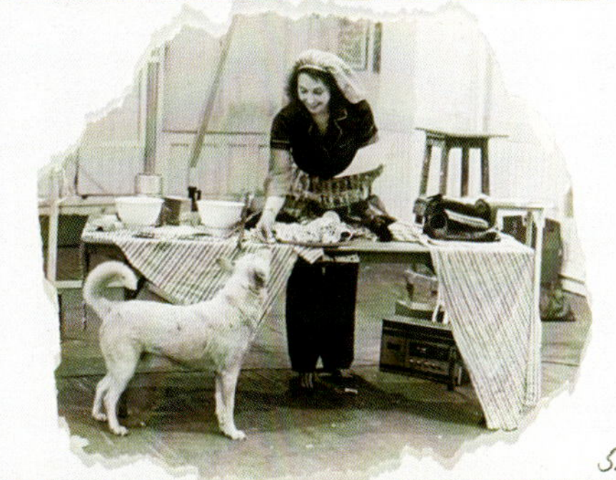

5.

always said: "People eat about 3 llbs of dirt every year." Now for the butterfly! Take bits of remaining pastry in yr fingers & flatten out-makes a vague sort of butterfly shape. Lay these over apples; pinch them onto edge of pastry on sides of dish. Keep laying the bits out until the top is covered. THAT'S ALL. Stick in oven. I do not "preheat" the oven because I think it gives a cruel shock to apples & flour & dish. Rather a nice gradual baking. Baking is like waiting for pubic

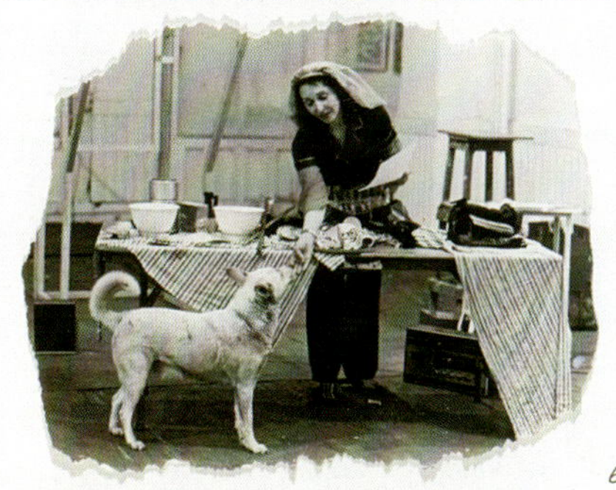

6.

hair to grow when yr 12 yrs old. Put it in & go away. Pretend nothing is happening. You will suddenly remember pies in the oven! Just in time to run,look, find they are still raw. Be patient & haughty. After a time you will see butter bubbling, smell absolute evidence....check pastry at bottom for crispness. Sample some. "mazing! Verdict: very sensuous & easy to do. Not up-tight making. A True Apple Pie. Archetypal. Serve to friends whose adoration you wish to bind forever.

30 BEATRICE WOOD

American, 1893–1997

a) *Gold Luster Plate*

1981
Earthenware
Diam: 13½ in.

b) *Copper Luster Chalice*

1989
Earthenware
H: 12¾ in.; W: 12 in.

Promised gifts of the Kira Fournier and Benjamin Schore Fund for Contemporary Sculpture

At the age of seventeen, Beatrice Wood fled her privileged life in New York to study art and theater in Paris, until she was forced to return home in 1916, following the outbreak of World War I. Back in New York, Wood befriended Henri-Pierre Roché, a French diplomat and art collector, and Marcel Duchamp, who introduced Wood to modern art and remained a close friend and source of inspiration for her throughout her life. Wood's artistic training began as an act of defiance toward her parents and continued as such in New York. Through her relationship with Duchamp, Wood was exposed to the avant-garde New York Dada group, and she eagerly assimilated its freewheeling spirit. She began sketching and drawing, imitating the styles of various contemporary artists and often including witty, erotic messages to accompany her drawings in the spirit of her Dada origins (Philp 1997). Wood was also associated with Walter and Louise Arensberg, influential collectors and patrons of modern art.

Wood did not come to ceramics until 1933, at the age of forty. After moving to Los Angeles, Wood enrolled in pottery classes at a local high school before studying with ceramicist Glen Lukens at the University of Southern California. In 1940, she worked with Austrian refugees Otto and Gertrud Natzler, who taught her how to use the wheel and introduced her to glaze chemistry. During this period she began to experiment with luster glaze. Dating back to ninth-century Mesopotamia, luster glaze is created by the presence of metallic salts on the surface of the glaze, which is fired in a specific manner in which oxygen is deliberately reduced during heating (Clark 1982). Breaking with the traditional methods of applying on-glaze luster, Wood experimented with and perfected the use of in-glaze luster, which added more depth and durability to the surfaces of her pieces. As a result, tiny breaks and iridescent streaks in the luster breathe life into the familiar, functional shapes for which she is known.

VVC

Clark, Garth. "Luster: The Art of Ceramic Light." In *Beatrice Wood Retrospective*. Fullerton: The MAIN Gallery, California State University, 1982. 31–38.

Naumann, Francis M. "The Drawings of Beatrice Wood." In *Beatrice Wood Retrospective*. Fullerton: The MAIN Gallery, California State University, 1982. 9–20.

Philp, Hunter Drohojowska. "Beatrice Wood: Still Making Art, and Mischief, After All These Years." *Art and Antiques* 3 (March 1997): 144.

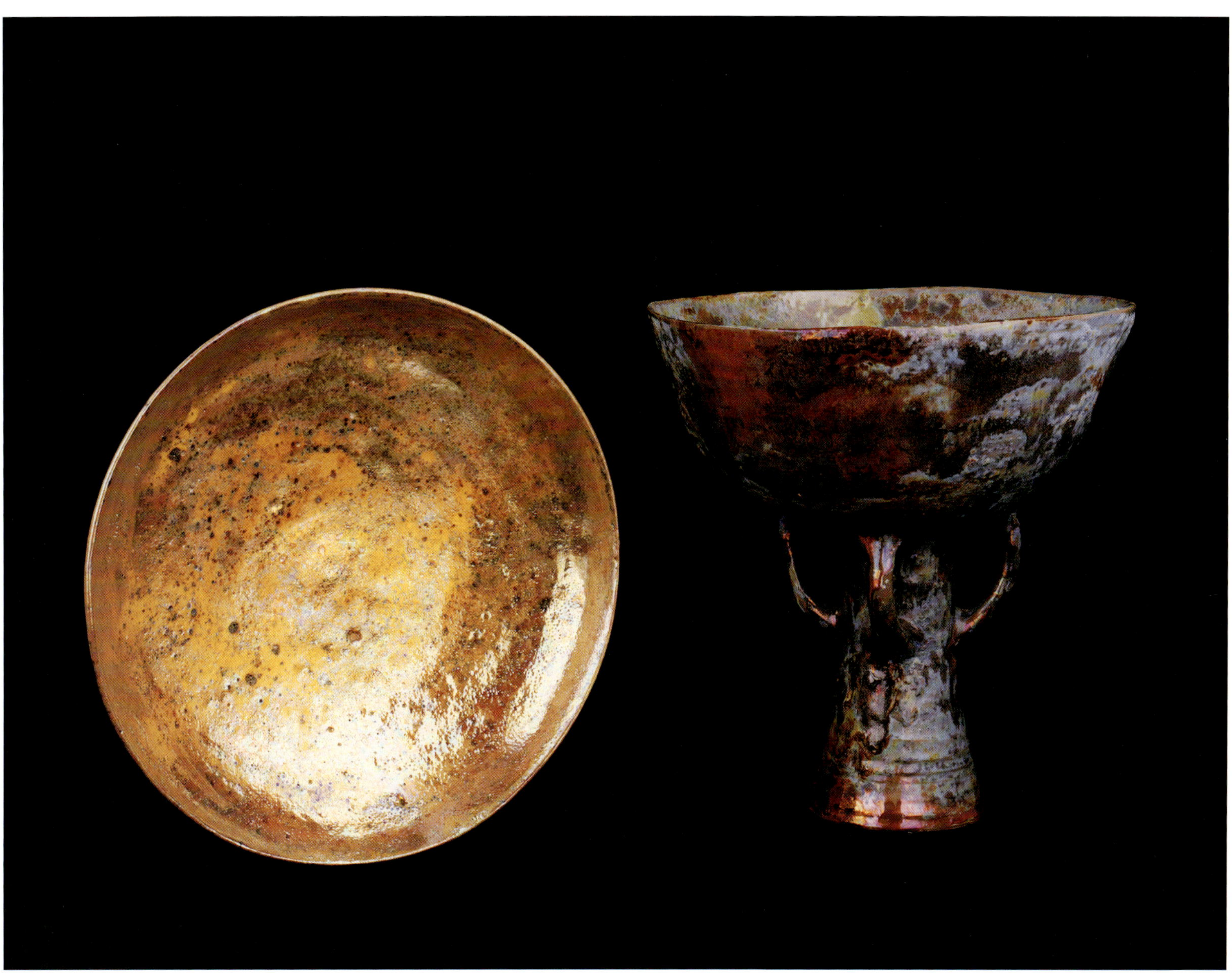

31 **CHUCK CLOSE**

American, born 1940

Phil II

Edition 1 of 15

1982

Paper pulp print on handmade paper

Published by Pace Editions Inc.

69 x 53½ in.

Promised gift of Richard J. Blum, Class of 1953

Image: Chuck Close, *Phil II*, handmade paper, ed. 11/15, 1982. Collection of Avampato Discovery Museum, Charleston, West Virginia. 1987 Museum Purchase funded by the Collectors Club.

Not in exhibition

Chuck Close claimed the attention of the art world in 1970 at his first solo show in New York, where he displayed a series of nine-foot-tall painted canvases of his friends as well as self-portraits. Since then, Close has focused on representing larger-than-life prints and paintings of the human face, or "heads," as he calls them. Although his subjects are almost always friends, fellow artists, family members, or himself, the monumental scale of his work forces the viewer to see the faces as ironically impersonal. In an affront to this impersonality, Close titles his heads with first names only. The effect is the opposite of the first-name titles used by Andy Warhol in prints such as *Marilyn*. Close creates an uneasy relationship between the intimacy of the titles and the abstract images of his sitters (Steiner 1987). Additionally, Close's use of the grid, which makes his artistic procedures visible on the surface of the painting, further removes the viewer from the space of the sitter (Kertess 1988).

Phil II is a paper pulp print of a friend of Close, the composer Philip Glass. Close created numerous prints of "Phil" in a variety of media based on the same photograph. He began the complex process by laying a grid over the photograph of Glass. On a much larger canvas, Close penciled in a larger grid that he numbered A1, B2, etc. Painting systematically from one side of the canvas to the other, Close created small abstract images that corresponded to what he saw in the small grids of the photograph. Using the large-scale watercolor image of Glass created in this manner, Close then worked with master printer Joe Wilfer and Dieu Donné Papermill to assign twenty-four shades of gray to the different colors in the watercolor picture. Next, a three-dimensional grid comprised of much smaller squares was laid over a large sheet of wet paper, each square having been numbered to correspond to a different grade of pigmented paper. The different shades of wet pulp were then squeezed through the squares onto the wet paper. This process was repeated several times, until a bunch of layers stacked up and were pressed together (Sultan 2003).

When *Phil II* is viewed up close, the small squares of paper pulp create tension between the immediacy of the image and the flat grids that make up the surface. Talking about the process of making these heads at the beginning of his career, Close stated, "The idea was to make something that was so large that it could not be readily seen as a whole and force the viewer to scan the image in a Brobdingnagian way, as if they were Gulliver's Lilliputians crawling over the surface of the face, falling into a nostril and tripping over a mustache hair" (Pelli 1999: F5).

VVC

Kertess, Klaus. *Chuck Close: New Paintings*. New York: Pace Gallery, 1988.

Pelli, Denis. "An Artist's Work Blurs Lines Between Art and Science." *New York Times*, Aug. 10, 1999, late ed.: F5.

Steiner, Wendy. "Postmodernist Portraits." *Art Journal* 46:3 (autumn 1987): 173–77.

Sultan, Terrie. *Chuck Close Prints: Process and Collaboration*. Princeton, NJ: Princeton University Press, in conjunction with Blaffer Gallery, the Art Museum of the University of Houston, 2003.

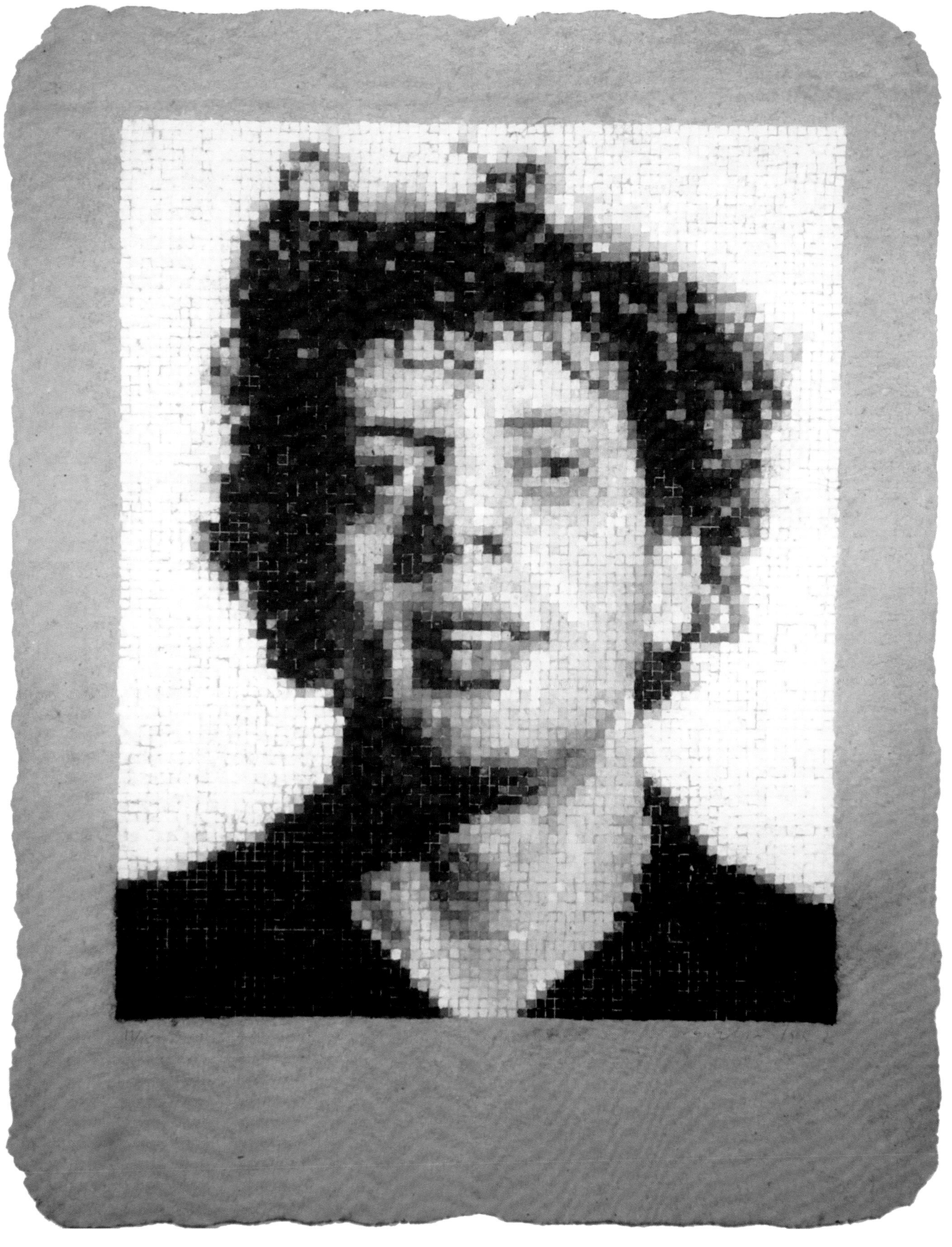

32 **TERRY WINTERS**
American, born 1949

Double Standard

Edition: 7/11
1984
Lithograph printed in twenty-two colors on Arches paper
Published by ULAE
78 x 42 inches

Gift of George T. M. Shackelford, Class of 1977, in honor of Sue and Duke Shackelford

Terry Winters's first solo exhibition of paintings at Sonnabend Gallery in New York coincided with the beginning of his foray into printmaking in 1982. Winters was invited to begin working in this process-oriented medium by Bill Goldston, who was head of the printmaking studio ULAE (Universal Limited Art Editions). Established in 1957 by Tatyana Grossman on Long Island, ULAE was one of the foremost print publishers at the time and had produced work by some of the most important New York artists of the late 1950s, 1960s, and 1970s, including Larry Rivers, Robert Rauschenberg, and Jasper Johns. Winters, who received his BFA from New York's Pratt Institute in 1971, started out as a minimalist painter, but by the early 1980s he had begun working with abstract organic forms that were rendered with a graphic sensibility. It is therefore not surprising that he favored lithography as the first printmaking process in which to work. Drawing had always been an integral part of Winters's work, and the lithography process allows the artist to work directly with a waxy crayon on the treated stone or plate.

Winters was inspired at the time by early botanical texts that contained illustration plates of various types of flora with marginalia revealing the plant at different stages of development. He played with this format in his paintings, drawings, and prints by placing smaller vignettes along the edges of the canvas or sheet. Also in keeping with a biological theme charting stages in a life cycle, his first five prints—*Ova, Factors of Increase*, and *Morula I, II, and III*—all include imagery suggestive of the fertilization and division of cells (a morula is a fertilized, dividing egg). In his sixth print, *Double Standard*, also a lithograph, Winters and his ULAE collaborators, Keith Brintzenhofe, John Lund, and Douglas Volle, created an immensely complex print that involving eighteen passes through two types of presses. The result is a richly layered image and the largest print ever made by the artist. This monumental work, unlike the others, captures the moment of fertilization, with spermlike forms penetrating spherical shapes that have veiled smaller honeycombed forms within their interiors. The multiple colors of the print—shades of black and gray, and a rusty brown—at first appear monochromatic but reveal their rich variation upon closer examination. The sheet contains all of the marks and smudges typical of a well-worked drawing, giving the sheet a vibrant immediacy and richness appropriate to its subject.

KWH

Ackley, Clifford S. "'Double Standard': The Prints of Terry Winters." *Print Collector's Newsletter* (U.S.A.) 18:4 (Sept.–Oct. 1987): 121–24, 5 illus.

Sojka, Nancy, with the assistance of Nancy Watson Barr. *Terry Winters Prints: 1982–1998: A Catalogue Raisonné*. New York: Hudson Hills Press, 1999.

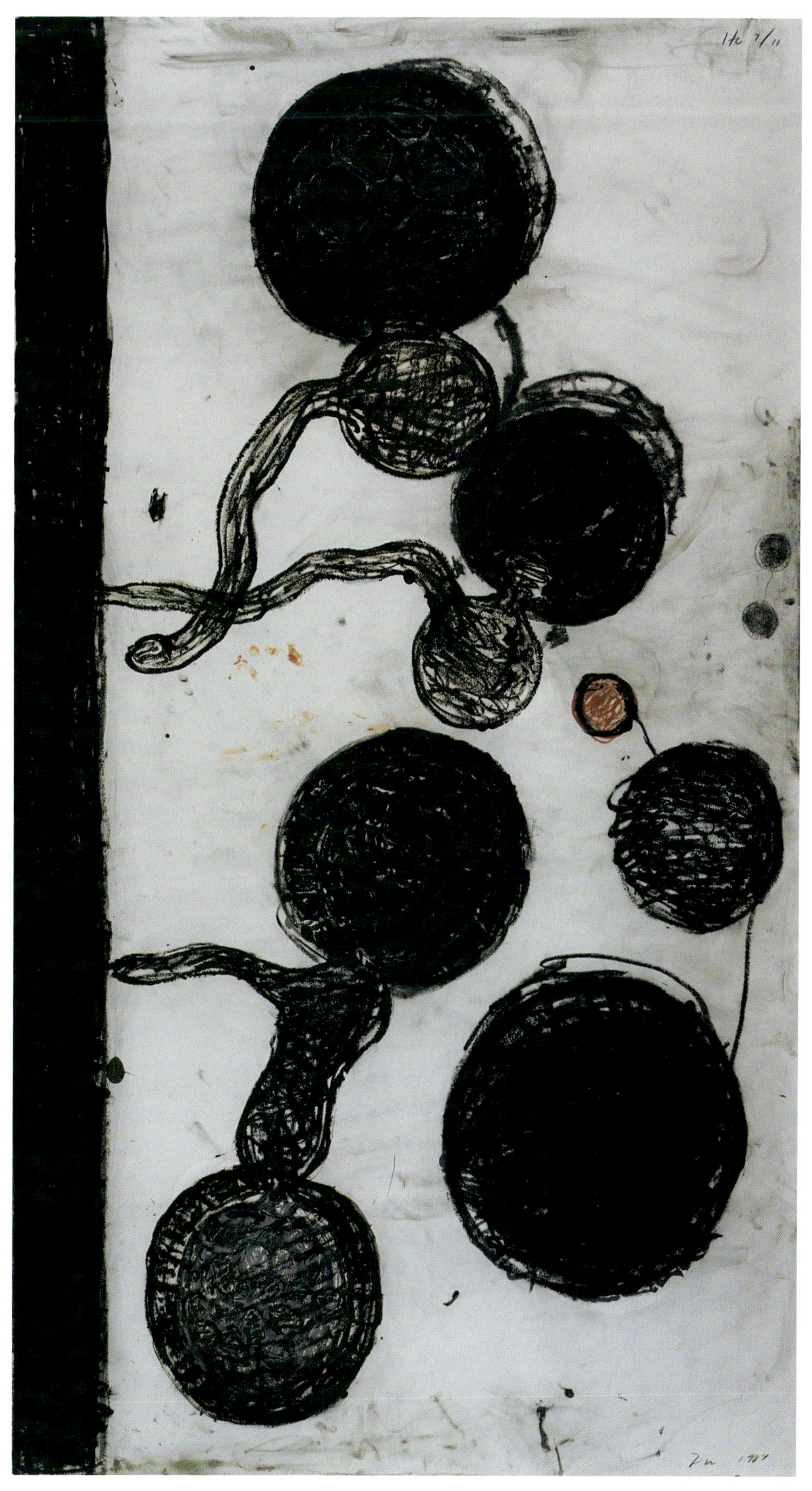

33 **JAMES NACHTWEY**

American, born 1948

San Miguel Province, El Salvador

1984
Color photograph
19 x 13 in.

Gift of Hugh J. Freund, Class of 1967

James Nachtwey, Class of 1970, one of the world's foremost photojournalists, has covered many of the conflicts and wars of the last quarter of the twentieth century, as well as those of the new millennium. He has been a tireless and active recorder of the horrors of war across the globe. He states: "I have been a witness, and these pictures are my testimony. The events I have recorded should not be forgotten and must not be repeated." His goal is to document the human dimension of war and the terrible manner in which it ravages not only the landscape and homes of civilian populations but also the bodies of both combatants and helpless bystanders caught up in the crossfire. Nachtwey has also brought international attention to the famines of Sudan and Ethiopia, the plight of Romanian orphans, the aftermath of the genocide in Rwanda, the consequences of AIDS on the African continent, and the corrosive industrial pollution of Eastern Europe.

Nachtwey's reputation comes in part from his continual presence at the very center of conflict and his ability to capture pictures that show, with heart-wrenching immediacy, the actions to which he is witness. This is conveyed by the great artistry of his work—his uncanny talent for composing and capturing an astonishing image in the midst of chaotic conditions. The stark beauty of his images frequently sits uneasily, in that their subject is human suffering. Their effectiveness, perversely, is dependent on his great skill as a photographer. His unrelenting focus on the consequences of war creates an intended discomfort in his audience, as it often goes beyond what is considered publishable or displayable in an art museum setting. These concerns are not important to him, as it is his intent to use his art to expose war's horror. To this end he published a compendium of his photographs from the 1990s, titled *Inferno*, and sent copies of the book to heads of state throughout the world.

Nachtwey taught himself the art of photography after graduating from Dartmouth College in 1970, where he studied political science and art history. His first professional assignment overseas was in 1981 in Northern Ireland, and soon after he covered the civil war in El Salvador. This image from that conflict shows a wounded child carried by a man, perhaps her father; in the background, a dead or wounded soldier is carried from the site. The standing figure in the back has extended the arm of the injured man as he lifts him off the ground, recalling a religious deposition, just as the two figures in the foreground appear as a Pietà. Often one does not have to know which side is being depicted in Nachtwey's photographs, only that the cost of human life is too high.

KWH

Nachtwey, James. *Deeds of War: Photographs.* Introduction by Robert Stone. New York: Thames and Hudson, 1989.

———. *Inferno/James Nachtwey.* London: Phaidon, 1999.

———. *James Nachtwey, Photojournalist.* Göteborg: Hasselblad Center, 1992.

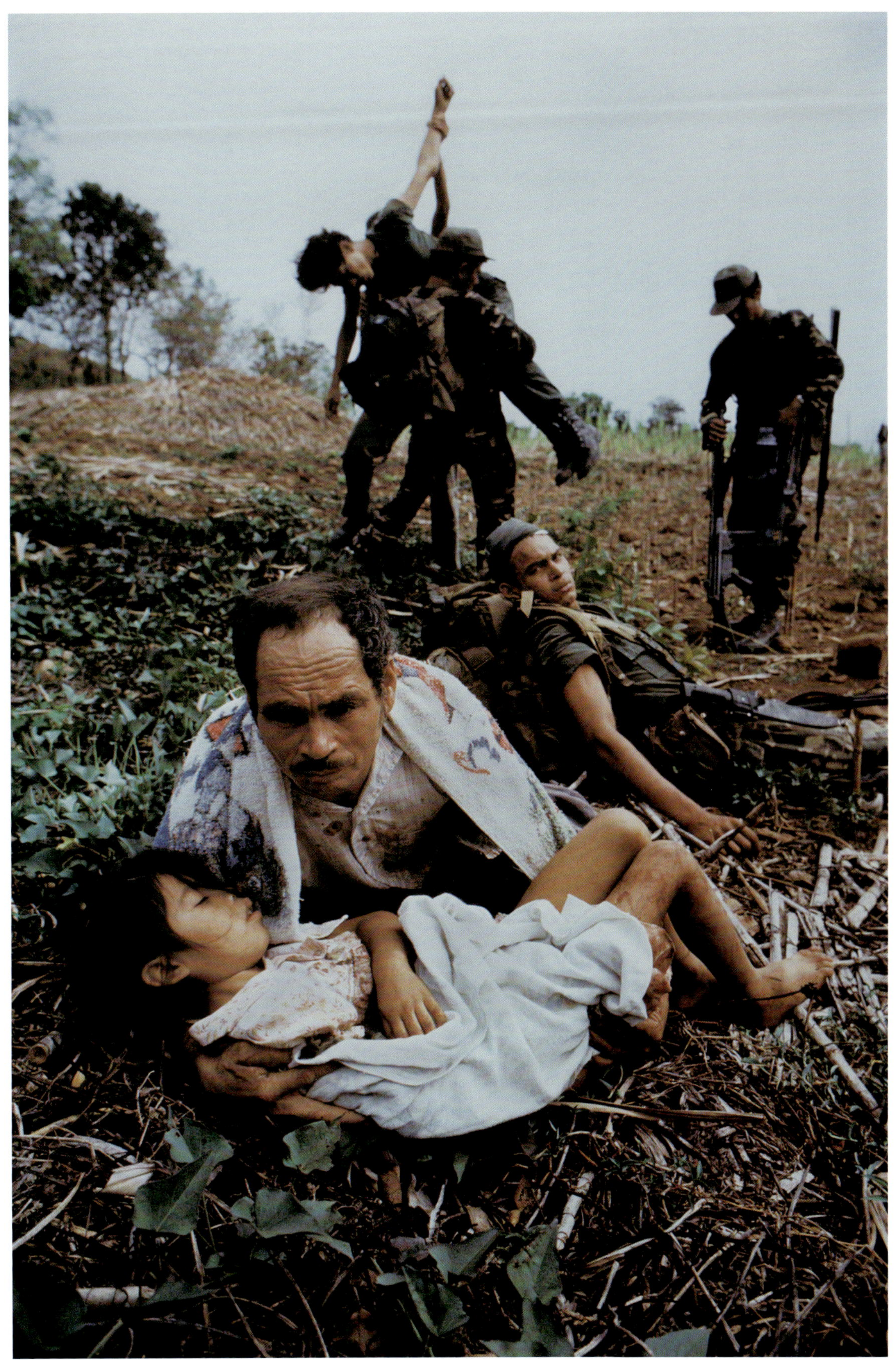

34 **SANDY WALKER**

American, born 1942

a) *These Mountains*

Edition 10 of 15
1986
Handprinted by John Stemmer on Kozo
30 x 22¼ in.

b) *Tree Ghost*

Edition 1 of 15
1987
Hand printed by John Stemmer on Suzuki
39¾ x 15 in.

Promised gifts of Robert Dance, Class of 1977

As a painter, Sandy Walker has worked extensively in black and white paint to create art that records his interaction with nature in a style that drifts between abstraction and representation. His embrace of this aesthetic of sharp contrasts has also found expression through his use of woodcut. As the oldest graphic technique, the woodcut process is a very direct and physical one—the artist carves away the negative space from the block and leaves the areas raised where he intends ink to appear on the print. Beginning with the German expressionists in the twentieth century, modern artists have adopted woodcut for its visual and psychological intensity. In his prints, Walker is able to create a sense of the immediacy and freedom of his experience with nature, despite the painstaking work that carving the woodblock entails.

These Mountains is one of Walker's darkest woodcuts. The block has been left almost entirely uncarved, with the negative space forming the abstracted outline of a mountain on the horizon. The grain of the wood shows through the dark stain of ink, standing witness to the former life of the artist's materials. The white forms of this print take on the appearance of spontaneous brushstrokes or ink blots, an effect that Walker achieves by first drawing outdoors on the blocks and then returning to the studio to carve into them. The disparity between the expressive record of his initial encounter with the natural world and the decisive finality of cutting into the wood parallels the coexistence of nature's constant energy and its gradual, measured rate of change.

In *Tree Ghost*, the artist pays homage to the tree. Katy Kline writes that, in general, Walker "venerates the tree as a potent totem of independent grandeur" (*Sandy Walker* 1994: 8). As in *These Mountains*, the carved-out white space here gives form to the image. Walker recognizes the irony inherent in his use of dead trees for both the blocks and the paper of his prints meant to venerate nature. In *Tree Ghost*, this paradox is emphasized as Walker presents the impression of a block from which he carved out and extracted the form of a tree. It is the shape of the wood that has been removed and discarded that creates the image of this tree spirit rising up grandly before the viewer. Throughout his work, Walker conveys a deep respect for the natural sources of both his inspiration and his materials.

MWL

Sandy Walker: Woodblock Prints. With an essay by Katy Kline. Cambridge, MA: MIT List Visual Arts Center, 1994.

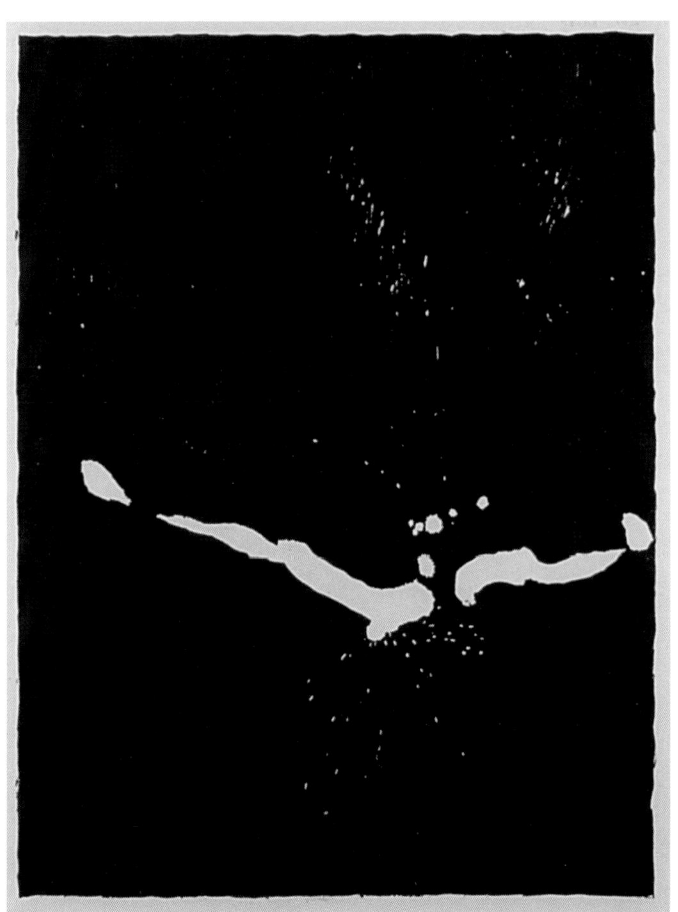

34a

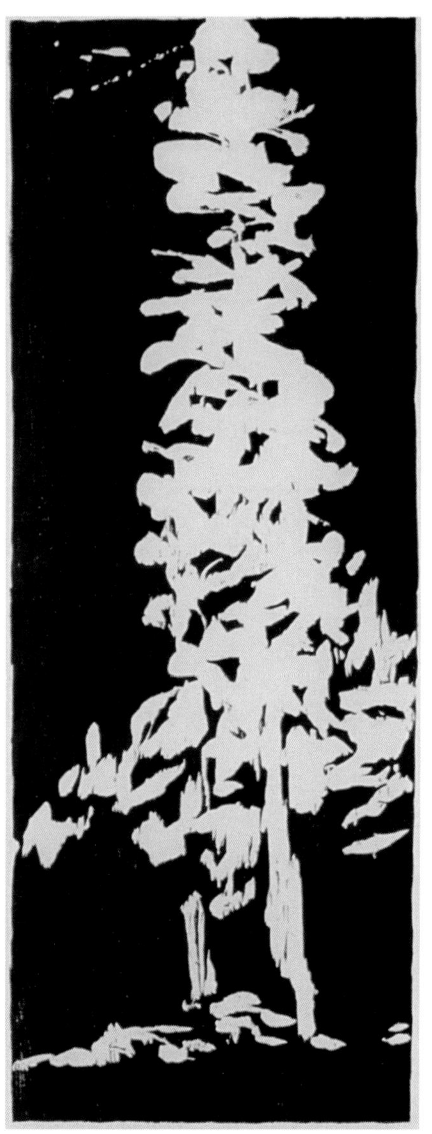
34b

35 **MAGDALENA UNGWANAKA**

Australian, birthdate unknown

Honey Ant Dreaming

1987
Acrylic on canvas
Frame: 23¾ x 35½ in.

Promised gift of Fannie and Alan Leslie M.D., Class of 1930, Medical School 1931

In Australia, the landscape carries spiritual and mythological significance based upon its origins in a corpus of epic stories referred to as Dreamings. These stories, which are recounted through storytelling, song, dance, and paintings, describe the lives and activities of ancestral beings, who traversed the Australian continent, creating the land, its people, and the cosmos, in an ancient period called the Dreamtime. During their journey across the land, these Dreamtime beings formulated laws for all living things to abide by. Each Dreaming describes how particular aspects of life and the known world came to be. Dreamings are therefore an important means of organizing, understanding, and constituting the significance of place and people in everyday Aboriginal life.

In this painting, Magdalena Ungwanaka, an artist most likely from the Hermannsburg–Finke River region of central Australia, represents the locations and activities narrated in the Honey Ant Dreaming, a well-known epic that is commonly featured in desert painting. Ungwanaka combines representational imagery of honey ants, a sweet-tasting insect that stores sucrose in its abdomen and is an Aboriginal source of nourishment, with abstract ideographs typical of central Australian desert painting. Ungwanaka liberally applies standardized symbols, such as small bars, ovals, concentric circles, footprints, and crescent shapes, to reference locations and activities that include honey ant colonies, water holes and rivers, ceremonial gatherings of people at campsites or around fires, human pathways, and sacred objects used in ceremonies—carrying dishes (*coolimon*), wooden clubs (*nulla-nulla*), shields, and digging sticks. While the specific symbols of the Honey Ant Dreaming depicted in this painting are not known, the painting more broadly represents the journey of the honey ants across their "country," or homelands, creating honey ant colonies along ancestral pathways established in the Dreamtime. These honey ant colonies can still be seen in the landscape today and are viewed as physical evidence of this epic journey.

BT

Dreamings of the Desert: Aboriginal Dot Paintings of the Western Desert. Adelaide: The Art Gallery of South Australia, 1996.

McCulloch, Susan. *Contemporary Aboriginal Art: A Guide to the Rebirth of an Ancient Culture*. Honolulu: University of Hawaii Press, 1999.

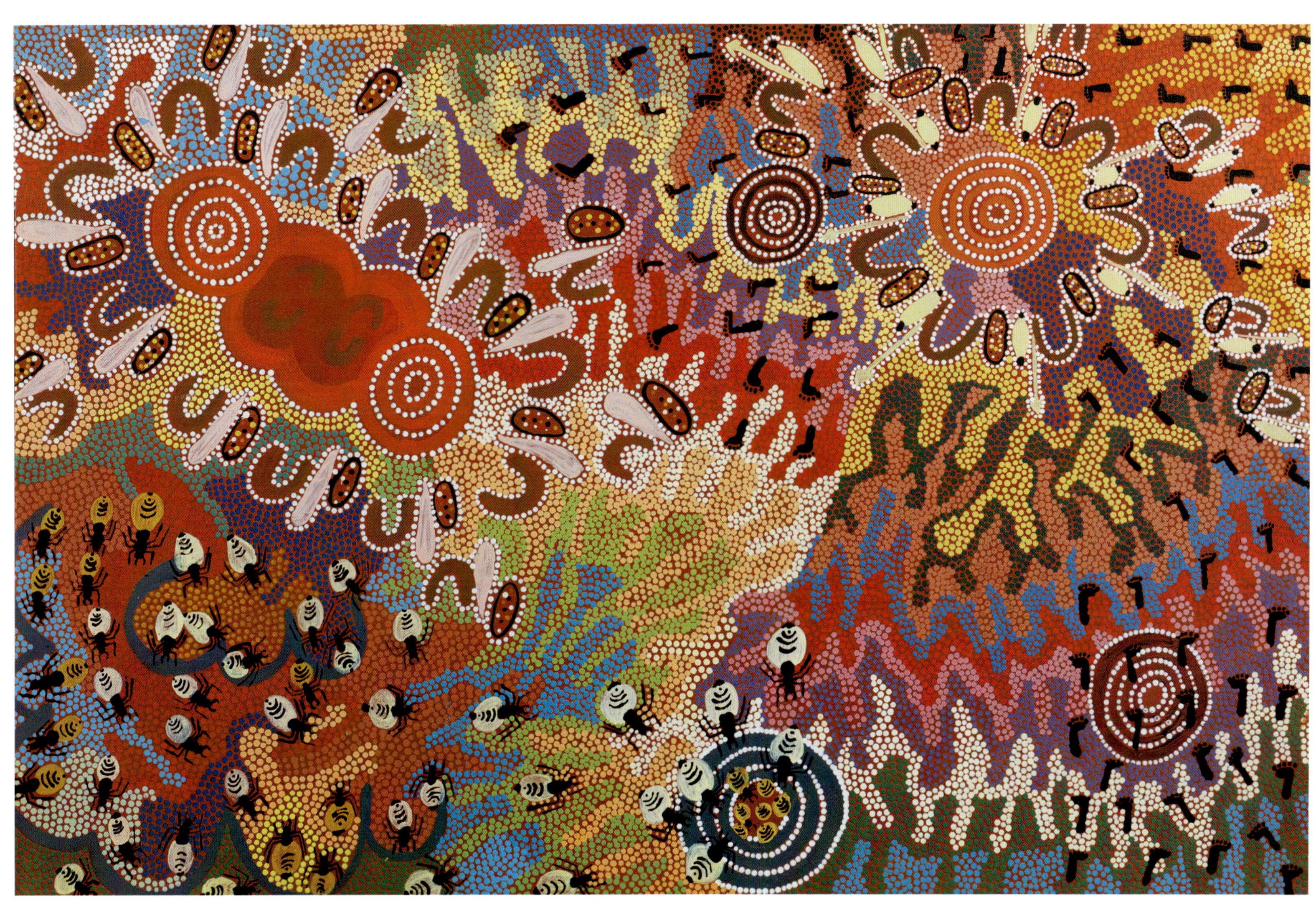

36 **ANDRES SERRANO**

American, born 1953

Piss Elegance

Edition 2 of 10

1987

Cibachrome, silicone, Plexiglas, wood frame

40 x 27½ in.

Promised gift from the Thomas F. O'Neil III Trust

Image courtesy Paula Cooper Gallery, New York

Andres Serrano's photographs are highly accomplished, ever-evolving, and always demanding of a visceral response in viewers. From his series *Bodily Fluids* of 1985–90, *Piss Elegance* teases out the link between attraction and repulsion to provoke conflicted responses from the interplay of its imagery, title, and material. In this, as in other works from the series, Serrano introduces the viewer to a situation that is full of contradictions and dichotomies, one where the sacred meets the profane.

Like Serrano's most controversial work, *Piss Christ*—which featured a color photograph of a Christ figure submerged in a glass of urine—*Piss Elegance* aims at something more than just shock effect. In this image, Serrano immerses a Venus figure in a tank filled with urine that is lit from behind and to the side to create a bright yellow, almost heavenly glow. The luminescence of the glowing urine serves as Serrano's point of departure in breaking down the object's materiality, and it creates a complex system of symbolism that reflects his own fascination with religious and sacred symbols, his ambivalent relationship with Catholicism, and his interest in metaphorically and emotionally charged bodily secretions, such as blood, milk, urine, and semen.

Early in his career, Serrano worked with religious imagery, but he then started to explore close-up photography of bodily fluids, removed from their usual context in a manner that referred to abstract, geometric, and action painting. The resulting imagery was very nonrepresentational and noncorporeal, which prompted the artist to return to the depiction of the human figure by submerging plastic figurines into his brightly lit containers filled with bodily fluids. In so doing, Serrano revisited the religious issues of his early years in a battle between beauty and the sublime.

BT

Hobbs, Robert, Wendy Steiner, and Marcia Tucker. *Andres Serrano: Works, 1983–1993*. Philadelphia: Institute of Contemporary Art, University of Pennsylvania, 1994.

Serrano, Andres, with Brian Wallis, ed. *Body and Soul: Andres Serrano*. New York: Takarajima Books, 1995.

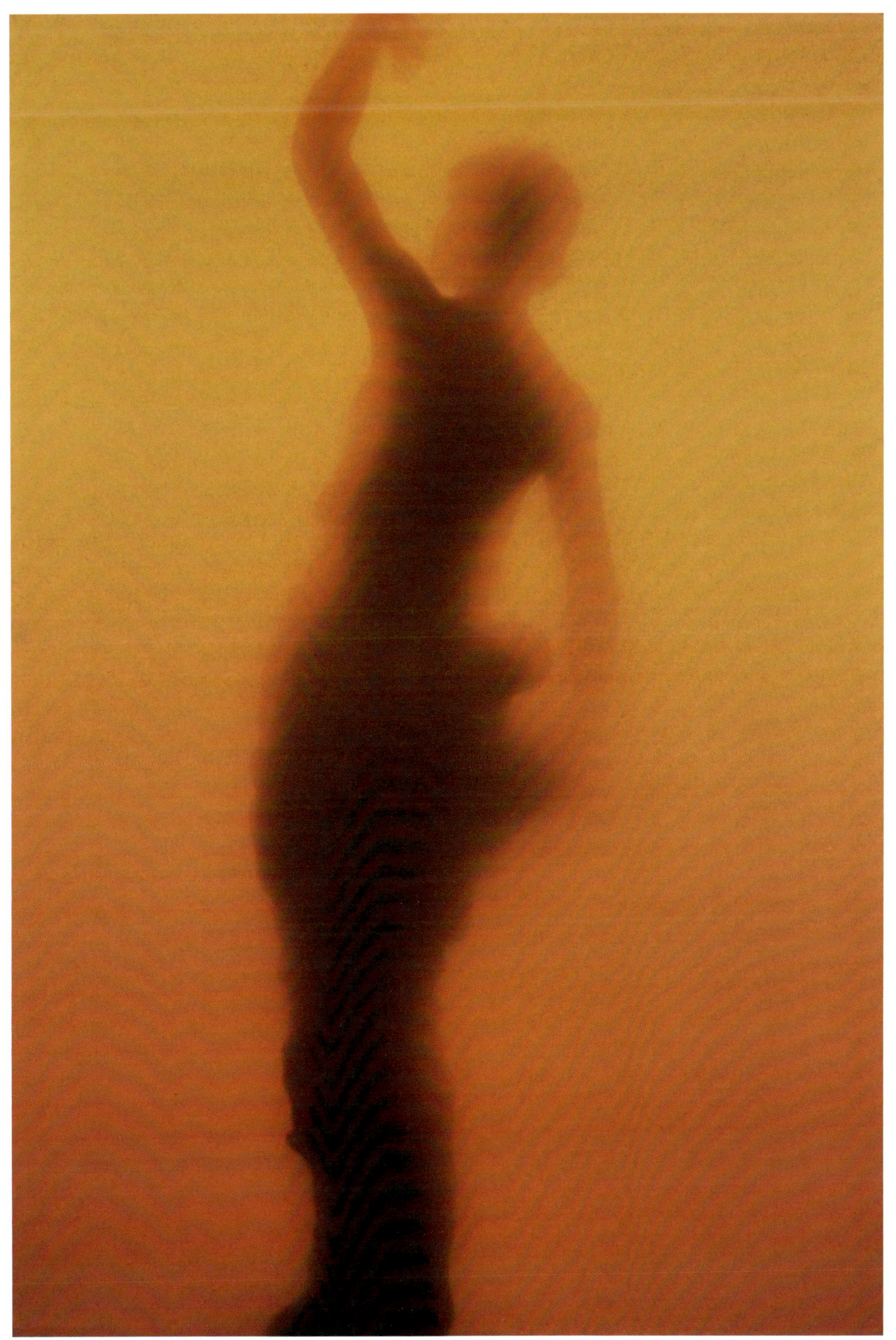

37 **RICHARD ERNST ARTSCHWAGER**

American, born 1923

Arch

1989
Wood and laminate
72 x 35¼ x 14⅜ in.

Donated by AXA Art Insurance Ltd., UK

Image courtesy Daniel Weinberg Gallery, Los Angeles

Richard Artschwager made furniture for a living in the 1950s after a brief stint in 1949–50 studying art under Amédée Ozenfant, a creator, along with Corbusier, of a cubist-inspired aesthetic of abstract forms and flat planes of monochromatic color called purism. Artschwager's interest in art continued during his years as a furniture maker, and he painted a series of landscapes in the late 1950s after the contents of his workshop were destroyed by fire, leaving him without the tools of his trade for an extended period. He made the transition to actively presenting himself as an artist in the early 1960s, when he began to make—perhaps inspired by the newly emerging pop art aesthetic of Jasper Johns and Claes Oldenburg—furniture-like forms painted with a false-grain pattern that imitated a wood surface. He soon began to apply to these sculptures a laminate veneer, making use of a commercial product called Formica. In a 1965 interview he stated, "It was Formica which touched it off. Formica, the great ugly material, the horror of the age, which I came to like suddenly because I was sick of looking at all of this beautiful wood." These easily recognizable everyday objects, with their exaggerated stocky forms and cheap imitation surfaces, took on an aggressive physicality with overtones of the pared-down aesthetic of minimalism and the idea-based framework of conceptual art, both of which were getting their start in the early 1960s. The conceptual aspect of Artschwager's work stems from the artist's engagement with the language of the universal in relation to the particular. He names his objects chairs, mirrors, or tables, but they are clearly less functional and more abstract, both monumental and sculptural in their sheer physicality.

Arch is clearly a descendent of these early works by the artist. It hangs on a wall but is sculptural in its projection from it. Its form originates from a Gothic-style arch, but when viewed from the side it also has the curved surface and jutting prow of a boat. Its formica-laminated frame is crisp, clean, and regular, but vastly rich in its repeated patterns of line, especially when compared to the flat black surface of its center. It mimics the "mirrors" that Artschwager intermittently created throughout his career, whose even, unreflective surfaces confuse those who stand in front of them and do not see their own reversed images. The sense of recognition that *Arch* and other Artschwager sculptures stir is immediately pushed aside by their obdurate refusal to fulfill the initial expectation that their form inspires.

KWH

Armstrong, Richard. *Richard Artschwager.* New York: Whitney Museum of American Art, in conjunction with W. W. Norton, 1988.

Schwarz, Dieter, ed. *Richard Artschwager: Texts and Interviews.* Winterthur: Kunstmuseum, 2003.

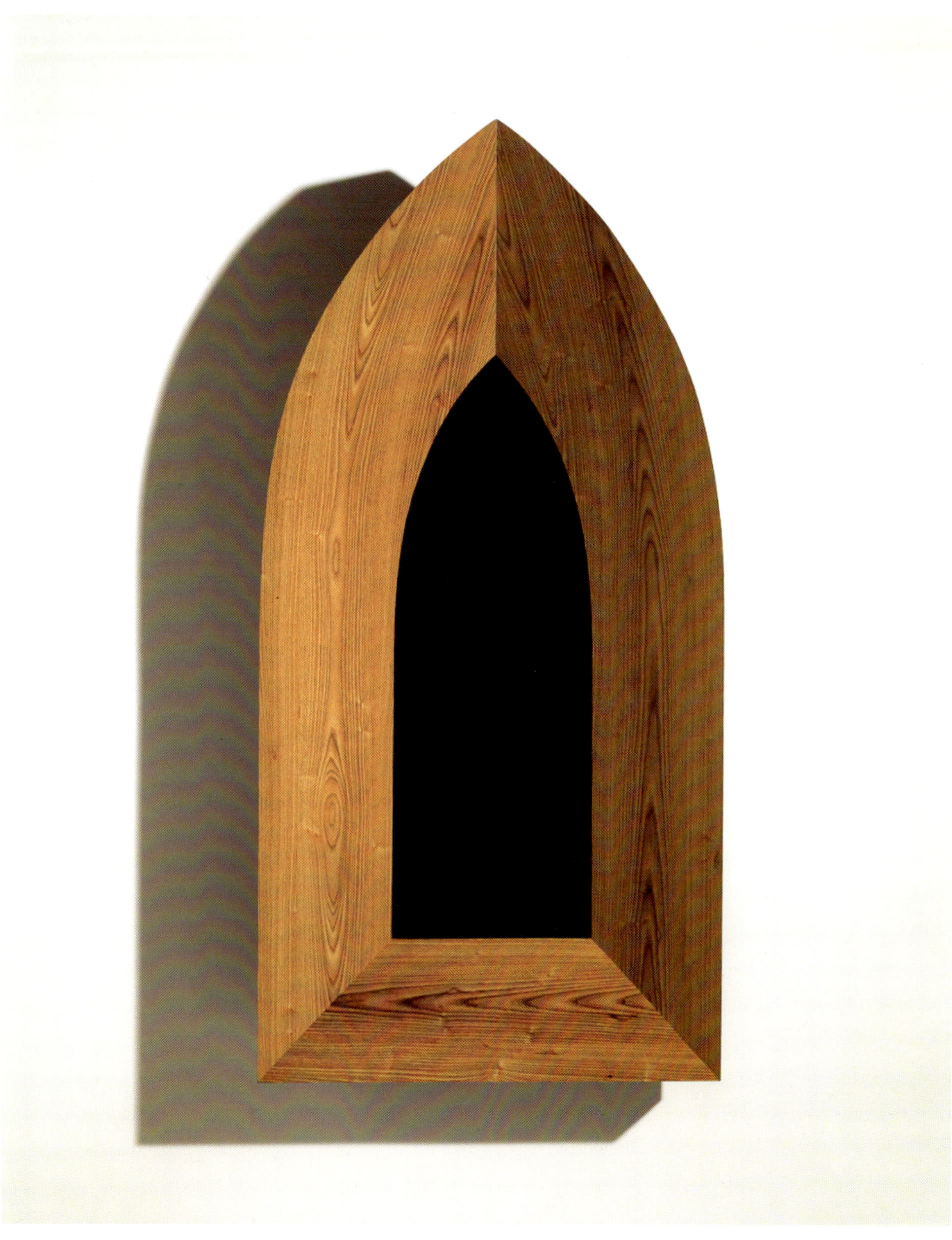

38 **JENNIFER BARTLETT**

American, born 1941

Fire-Table I

1989

Oil on canvas and enamel on wood

84 x 60 in. (painting), H: 32⅞ in. (table)

Gift of Sondra Gilman and
Celso M. Gonzalez-Falla

Jennifer Bartlett first entered onto the contemporary art scene in the early 1970s with installations of small steel plates coated with a white baked enamel, painted with fastidious configurations of dots, and then organized in grids. These pieces launched her career but certainly have not defined it. Throughout the 1970s and 1980s, her work evolved away from the obsessive control so central to these early installations to embrace a painterly depiction of nature. And while her minimalist grids had emphasized the flatness of the wall, Bartlett also began to include sculptural elements that created a much different three-dimensional experience for viewers.

In 1989, Bartlett presented a show at the Paula Cooper Gallery in New York titled *Fire Paintings*. The works all featured painted canvases with objects on the floor before them. Throughout the series, a bright orange fire rages that does not consume but instead energizes the natural world around it. As in *Fire-Table I*, Bartlett depicted clean and simple manmade objects within her compositions in opposition to the heated wildness. Here, it is an orange hexagonal table, which was one of the items depicted throughout *Fire Paintings*. The same table stands in front of the canvas in three-dimensional form, scaled and positioned to directly correspond to its painted version. This extends the scene into the viewer's space, creating a jarring disjunction between the quiet peacefulness of the gallery that the sculpture inhabits and the apocalyptic vision contained in the canvas.

MWL

Cyphers, Peggy. "Paula Cooper Gallery, New York; exhibit." *Arts Magazine* 64 (April 1990): 111.

Goldwater, Marge, Jennifer Bartlett, Roberta Smith, and Calvin Tomkins. *Jennifer Bartlett*. Minneapolis: Walker Art Center, 1985.

Jennifer Bartlett: Recent Work. Introduction by D. Sobel. Milwaukee: Milwaukee Art Museum, 1988.

Kalina, Richard. "Paula Cooper Gallery, New York; exhibit." *Art in America* 78 (April 1990): 261–62.

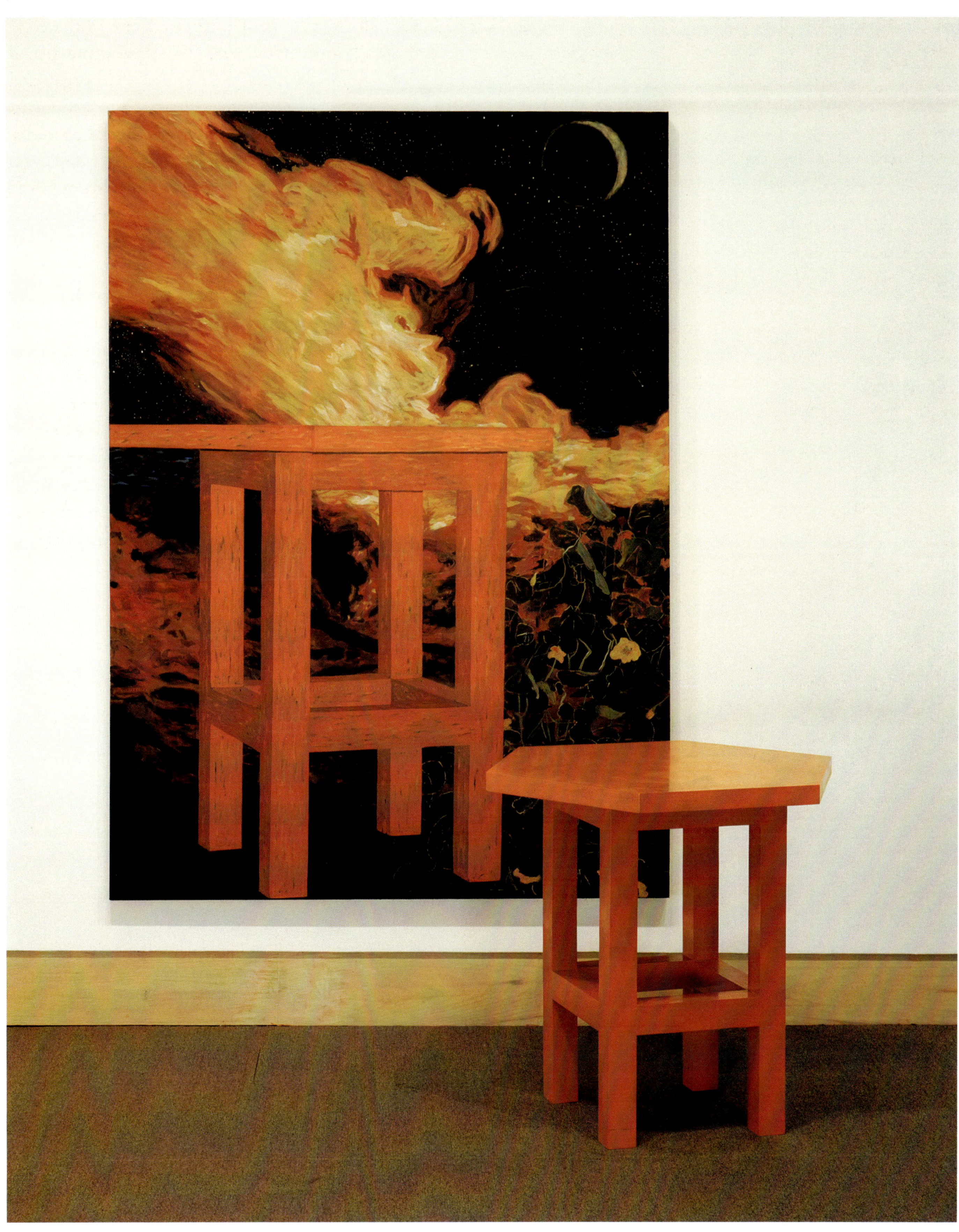

39 **PANSY MARTIN NAPANGARDI**

Australian, born 1949

Untitled

1990
Acrylic on canvas
36 x 53 in.

Gift of Madeleine and Stephen Lister, Class of 1963

In the early 1970s, a new era in Australian history began with the exodus of Aboriginal peoples back to their ancestral homelands after two hundred years of European Australian domination, cultural suppression, and segregation. From this exodus emerged a new art movement, in which Aboriginal artists adopted acrylic painting on canvas to assert, preserve, and express their rights, cultural identity, and kinship to the Australian land. In visual representations of sacred epics called Dreamings, Aboriginal artists embedded symbolic imagery and iconography with reaffirmations of their native rights and cultural connections to the land, emphasizing as well the land's importance to their cultural survival and preservation. However, the abstract quality, cryptic icons, and esoteric meanings inherent in these contemporary paintings make it difficult—if not impossible—for outsiders to decipher the specific meanings of the imagery, which is restricted to Aboriginals who own the rights to each Dreaming.

Born in Haasts Bluff to a Walpiri father and Luritja mother, Pansy Martin Napangardi lived her youth in the local mission settlement and was later resettled to the Papunya reserve in 1960. In the early 1970s, at the start of the new painting movement in Papunya, Napangardi began depicting her Dreamings in the sand under the guidance of her grandmother and grandfather. From sand painting she later ventured into acrylic painting, all the while observing other well-known Papunya artists, who had by then established the specific Papunya style of painting. This style is characterized by the use of muted earth tones and ocher colors, primarily yellow, white, black, and red, as well as geometric bands of color and symbolic icons of dotted shapes, connected or outlined by contrasting lines and curvilinear patterns. Since moving to Alice Springs in 1989, Napangardi's experimental nature and close contact with non-Aboriginal Australians have helped her develop a hybrid style that fuses her Aboriginal heritage with a contemporary urban sensibility. She is now regarded as one of the foremost Papunya artists in Alice Springs.

BT

Dreamings of the Desert: Aboriginal Dot Paintings of the Western Desert. Adelaide: The Art Gallery of South Australia, 1996.

McCulloch, Susan. *Contemporary Aboriginal Art: A Guide to the Rebirth of an Ancient Culture.* Honolulu: University of Hawaii Press, 1999.

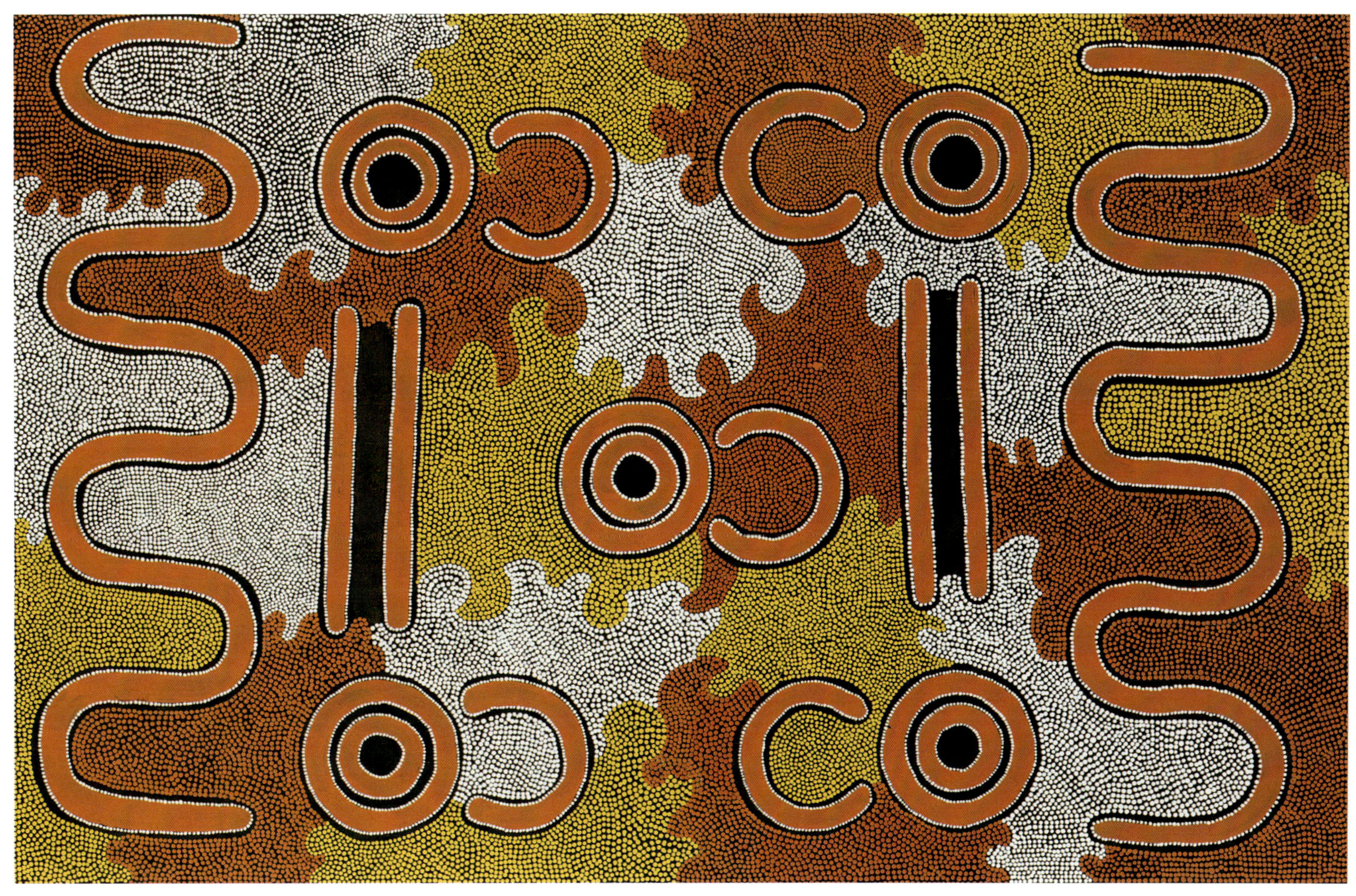

40 **ROBERT STIVERS**

American, born 1953

All works from *Series 5*, gelatin silver prints, 10 x 8 in., artist's proof #1 (numbered edition of 10)

a) *Arm & Hand #1*
1996
Gift of Jamie and Haim Handwerker

b) *Chair*
1996
Gift of Bart Osman, Class of 1990, Tuck 1996

c) *Leg*
1996
Gift of Scott Osman, Class of 1980

d) *Seated Man*
1988/1994
Gift of Bart Osman, Class of 1990, Tuck 1996

e) *Spine*
1996
Gift of Jamie and Haim Handwerker

f) *Wrapped Woman* (illustrated)
1994
Gift of Bart Osman, Class of 1990, Tuck 1996

Robert Stivers made the decision to become a photographic artist in 1988. Previously, he had pursued a career as a professional dancer, performing as a member of the Joffrey Ballet company, but a serious back injury forced him to stop dancing. He turned to the business world next, working as an insurance agent and stockbroker, but he eventually decided that he needed to find a new creative and artistic outlet. At the age of 35, he settled on photography and registered for courses at UCLA. He studied the work of other artists, learned about the specifics of photographic technology, and experimented with the medium, eventually discovering his own aesthetic sensibility in the 1990s. His style is one characterized by out-of-focus forms that rise, as if through a mist, to the surface of the prints. One critic finds in Stivers's work "a world where amorphous forms emerge out of formlessness to become distinct for a brief time before folding back into a kind of eternal void" (Pitnick 2001).

All of the photographs included in this exhibition, including *Wrapped Woman*, which is illustrated here, come from Stivers's *Series 5*. They were published together as his first book, titled *Robert Stivers: Photographs*, in 1997. The images are hauntingly ethereal, with blurry body parts, inanimate objects, animals, and contorted bodies seemingly emanating light out of the deepest possible darkness. Particularities are blended away by the shadows and Stivers's play of chemicals in the darkroom to produce mysterious, nearly abstract forms that seem to exist more in a spiritual than a physical world. The figure in *Wrapped Woman* is like a ghostly apparition—her brightly exposed face, with its dark holes for eyes, is both disturbing and beautiful. The calmness of her expression seems strange considering the tight wrap that envelops her. Such tensions—between peace and anxiety, beauty and horror, presence and absence—appear throughout Stivers's work and make his images disquieting yet compelling.

MWL

Pitnick, Richard. "Spotlight: Robert Stivers." *Black & White Magazine* 13 (June 2001).

Rollins, Ron. "Robert Stivers and His Artistic Influences: Seemingly Obvious, but Only at First." http://www.wright.edu/artgalleries/.

Stivers, Robert. Artist's personal Web site. http://www.robertstivers.com.

———. *Photographs*. Santa Fe: Arena Editions, 1997.

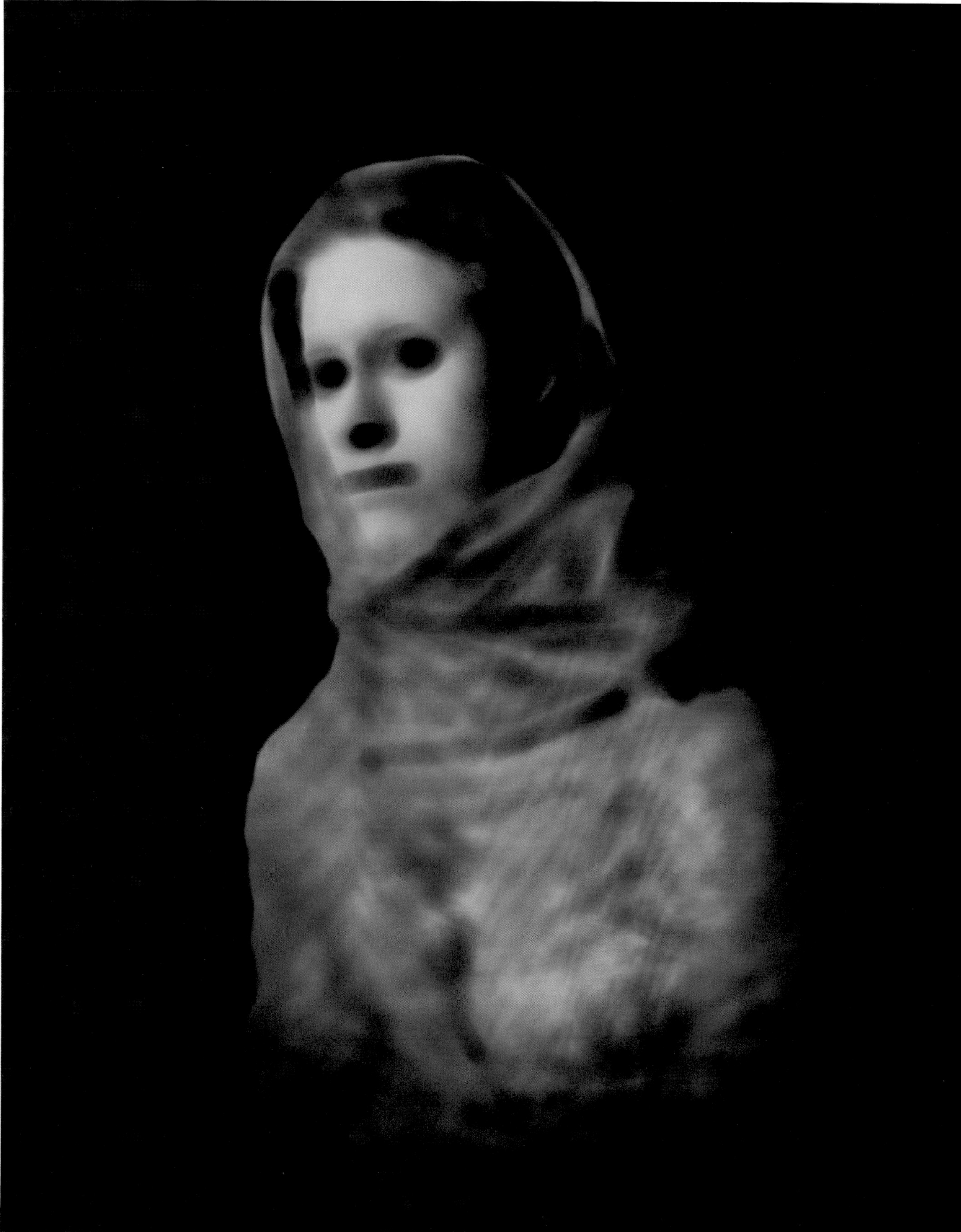

41 **EDWARD BURTYNSKY**

Canadian, born 1955

Shipbreaking #31, Chittagong, Bangladesh

2000

Dye-coupler print

34 x 27 in.

Gift of Jane and Raphael Bernstein

Image courtesy of Charles Cowles Gallery, New York

Edward Burtynsky has been documenting industrial landscapes of the modern world for the past twenty years. His photographic essays of mining, quarrying, railcutting, recycling, oil refining, and shipbreaking portray the fragile balance between man and the environment. The subjects in his photographs are often highly dynamic, being both complex symbols of man's interaction with the landscape and mesmerizingly beautiful images. This dualism between form and content is important to Burtynsky's work (Torosian 2003). He often refrains from editorializing on his apocalyptic images; instead he allows viewers to ponder the aesthetics or the politics of the picture as they please.

Shipbreaking is a process of industrial recycling that can only take place in locations where the land and the sea meet in such a way that large ships can be beached. Because of environmental hazards, shipbreaking typically occurs in developing and economically challenged countries, where the need for inexpensive steel outweighs the dangers of the process. Burtynsky's *Shipbreaking #31* recalls the sublime paintings of Turner and Friedrich that spoke to a world coping with the effects of the Industrial Revolution. Like the nineteenth-century landscape photographers he admires, Burtynsky uses a large-format viewfinder camera to create highly detailed images that show a depth of clarity that the naked eye could not recreate. Speaking about his formal approach to photography, Burtynsky said, "Often my approach, the compression of space through light and optics, also yields an ambiguity of scale. You don't know how large anything is until you see a detail whose size you can recognize. Then you have to reconstruct reality to comprehend how big the place really is . . . our presence is dwarfed by the spaces we've created" (Torosian 2003: 52–53). In *Shipbreaking #31*, a lone figure running toward the shore almost disappears, a human presence that cannot compete with the imposing size of the ship and the vastness of the sea. The man, barefoot and casually dressed, is ironically juxtaposed against a ruin of man's industrial achievement.

VVC

Hannon, Gerald. "The Eyes of Ed Burtynsky." *Toronto Life* 38:2 (February 2004): 80.

Torosian, Michael. "The Essential Element: An Interview with Edward Burtynsky." In *Manufactured Landscapes: The Photographs of Edward Burtynsky*, ed. Lori Pauli. Ottawa: National Gallery of Canada, in conjunction with Yale University Press, 2003. 46–55.

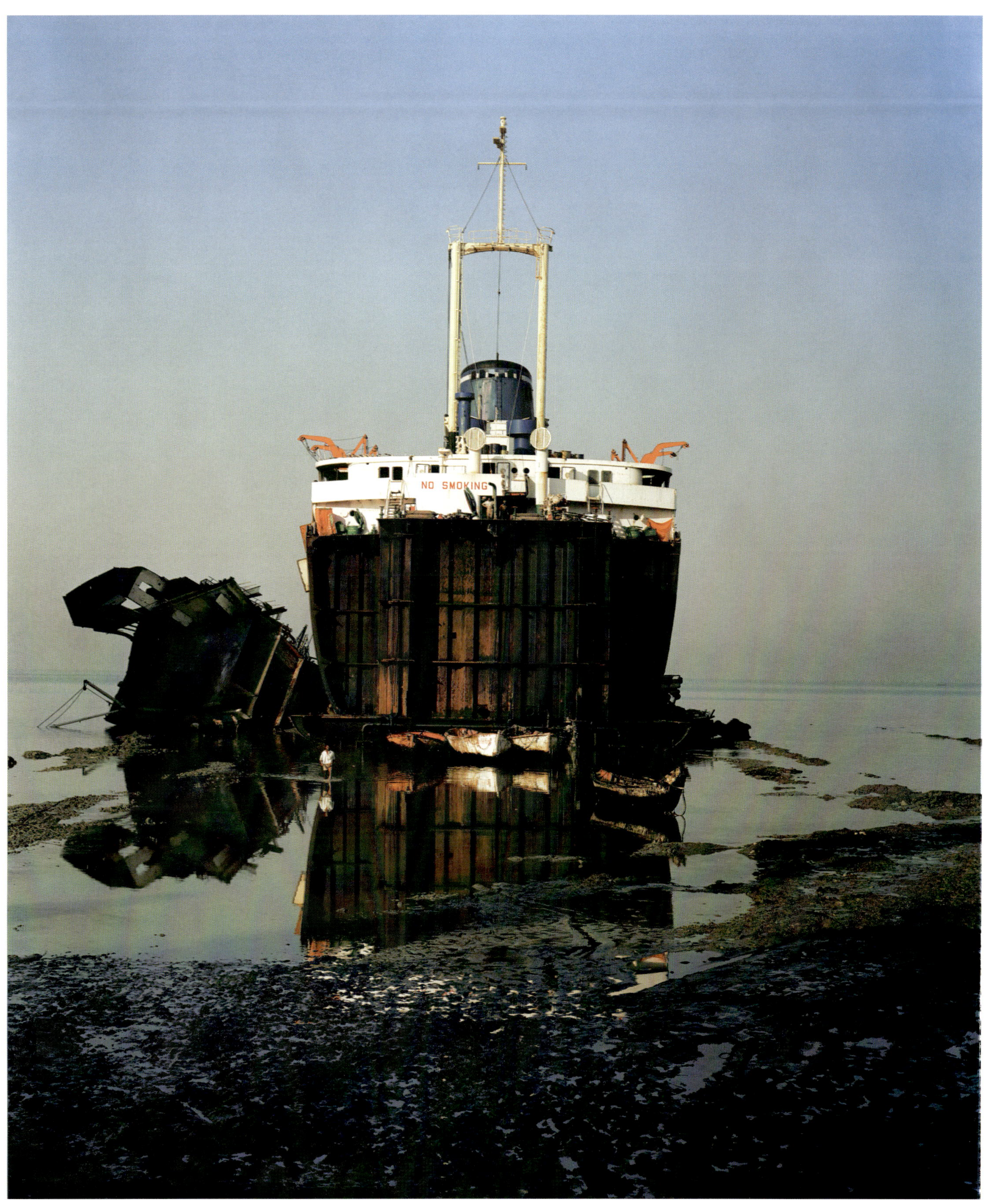
NO SMOKING

42 **KATHLEEN GILJE**

American, born 1945

A Voice Cries Out in the Wilderness, Restored

2001
Oil on canvas
30 x 25 in.

Promised gift of Robert Dance, Class of 1977

John the Baptist is depicted here as a three-quarter-length figure staring aggressively out at the spectator while holding a muddy lamb in his lap and a reed staff crudely fashioned as a cross in one hand. His right hand points assertively at the cross, which foretells the crucifixion of Jesus. The compact format, outward gaze, dramatic lighting, and vivid illusionism—highlighted by the plasticity of the red cloak wrapped around his body—intensify the impact of the striking image.

Freshly tattooed on John's right shoulder are the words "A Voice Cries Out in the Wilderness." The same composition, without the tattoo, was painted by Antonio d'Enrico, called Tanzio da Varallo (ca. 1575–ca. 1632). This early baroque artist is renowned for his combination of the elegant mannered style of his native Lombardy and the realism introduced by his near-contemporary Caravaggio.

Kathleen Gilje has reinterpreted—or creatively "restored"—Tanzio's unconventional depiction of the youthful saint. The Gospels describe John the Baptist as the herald for the coming Christ. As a late adolescent he left home for the wilderness to prepare for his ministry. "A Voice Cries Out in the Wilderness" refers to John's period of isolation, but its companion verse, "Prepare the way for the Lord," also announces the advent of the Messiah, a key event in the Christian notion of salvation. With this first phrase (which is also a translation of the official motto of Dartmouth College) boldly emblazoned on his upper arm, the juvenile is stirred not so much by divine inspiration as by streetwise toughness. Gilje has subtly transformed the baroque artist's message of salvation to one of contemporary confrontation.

Gilje's painting is convincingly rendered with the same materials and handling as those used in the original picture executed nearly four hundred years earlier. Although her technical skill was acquired through years of practice as a conservator, she demonstrates a powerful aptitude for bringing new meaning to old masterpieces.

TBT

Nochlin, Linda. "Seeing Beneath the Surface." *Art in America* 90:3 (March 2002): 118–21.

Williams, Gregory. "Kathleen Gilje." *Artforum International* 40:3 (November 2001): 147.

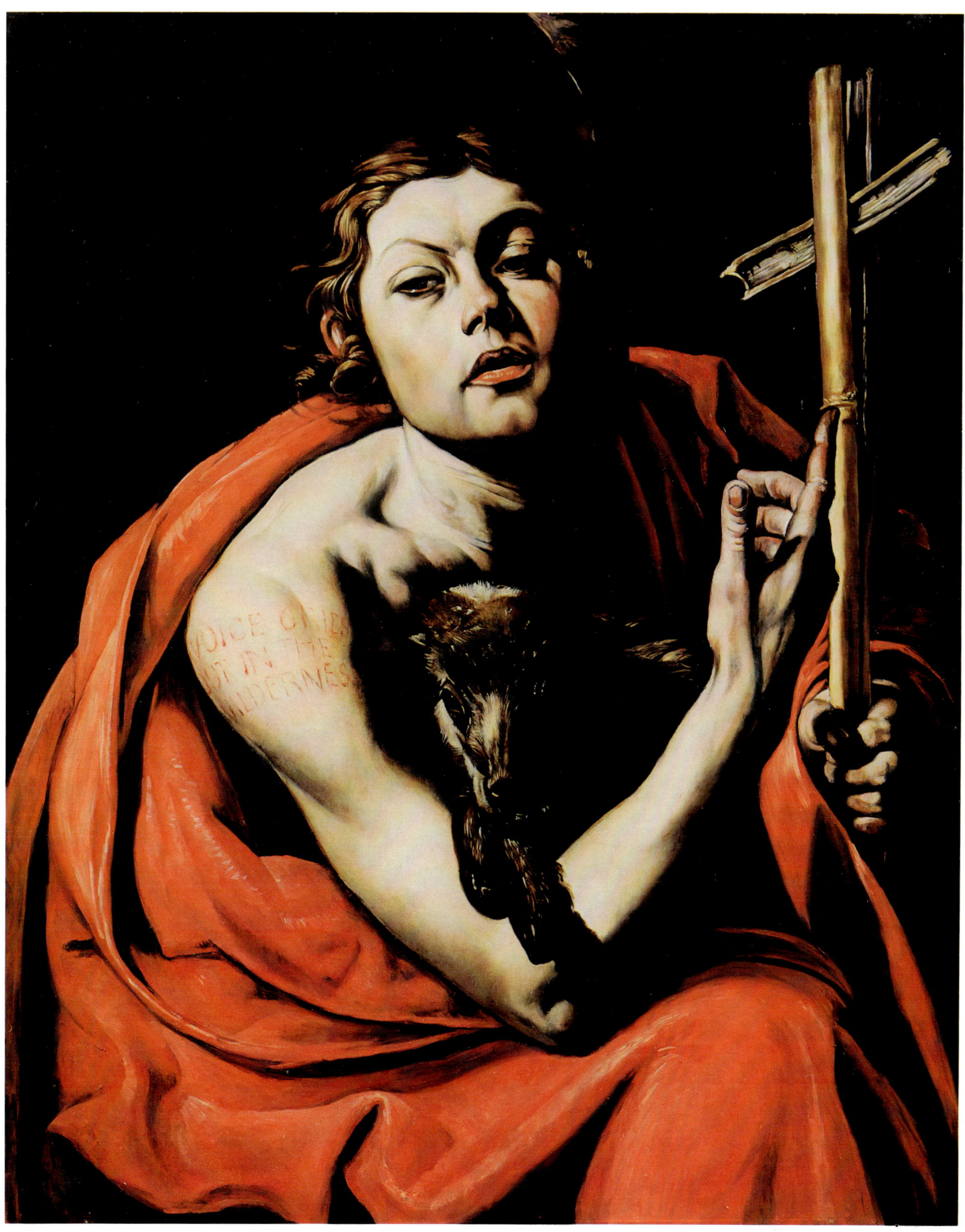
VOICE
IN THE

43 **SZE TSUNG LEONG**

American and British, born 1970

Chaotianmen, Yuzhong District, Chongqing

Edition 1 of 6
2002
Chromogenic color print
Image: 32 x 40 in.

Promised gift of Andrew E. Lewin, Class of 1981

Image courtesy of the artist

Sze Tsung Leong was trained at Berkeley and Harvard as an architect and is presently based in New York. In 2001, he decided to set aside his architectural practice in order to pursue an ambitious photographic project to document the changing face of China's cities. China's urban regions have seen a particularly accelerated rate of change over the last two decades. As Chinese society has moved to embrace Western capitalism, cities have drawn in twenty million people each year through the promise of new employment. Consequently, huge renovation projects have been initiated that typically involve the destruction of older buildings, with generic, utilitarian structures taking their place. Leong writes, "Presently in China, history as urban form is seen in contradictory terms: as proof of China's accomplishments and contributions to civilization, yet more often as an inconvenience to urban modernization" (Leong 2004: 19). According to Leong, his series *History Images* is a record of histories in the process of being erased, the absence of histories (in the form of entirely razed sites), and future histories that are yet to take place within the newly constructed environments.

In *Chaotianmen, Yuzhong District, Chongqing* we see a pier jutting out into the part of the Sichuan basin where the Yangtze and Jialing rivers meet. Chaotianmen has historically been a very important port, as it is the first dock on the Yangtze, and the city of Chongquing has grown immensely in recent years. In the photograph, we see its modern skyscrapers rising through the thick fog that is a typical feature of the region's climate. The dim outline of the skyline gives one the sense that this could be just the vision of a possible reality rather than a concrete record of the present. The buildings appear fuzzy and almost transparent, and it is only the colorful pier that is brought into focus. At least for outsiders, this long, thin, slightly curved pier is reminiscent of images of the Great Wall, arguably China's best known historical structure, and so it provides a reminder of the past that is being replaced. Because of the vantage point Leong chooses, viewers are given the sense that this pier could lead away from the city indefinitely—perhaps providing an escape route for the tiny human figures who walk along it, dwarfed by the manmade immensity that ascends behind them.

MWL

Grundberg, Andy. "Between Past and Future: New Photography and Video from China." *Aperture* 177 (winter 2004): 12–14.

Leong, Sze Tsung. "History Images." *Art Journal* 63:4 (winter 2004): 19, 22–45.

Phillips, Christopher. "Drastic Urbanization: The Photographs of Sze Tsung Leong." *Art Journal* 63:4 (winter 2004): 20–21.

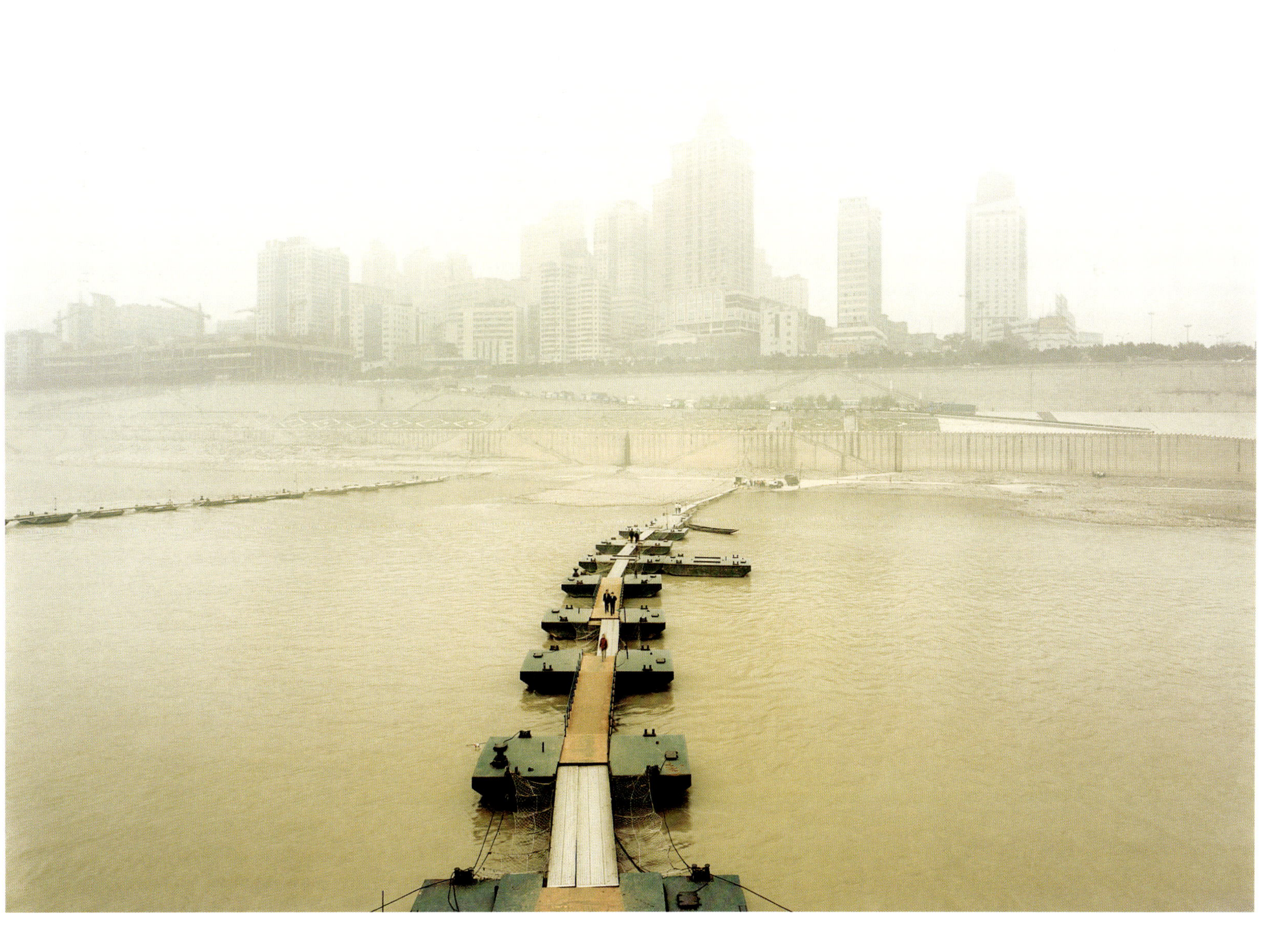

44 **PAUL CHAN**

born 1973 in Hong Kong

Buildings as Monuments as Graves 2

Edition 1 of 5 plus 3 artist's proofs
2003
Inkjet print on archival paper
44 x 78 in.

Promised gift of Monroe Denton, Class of 1968, in honor of Derrick Cartwright, Director of the Hood Museum of Art, 2000–2004

Image courtesy Greene Naftali Gallery, New York

Paul Chan is an artist and political activist working in diverse new media who associates himself with outsider art, which he defines as the "embrace of established forms and traditions" that is "so tight that it threatens to collapse the forms themselves in a suffocating excess, and in the process, transform the very traditions that elevated those forms in the first place" (Chan, "Sublime Humility"). Chan's *Buildings as Monuments as Graves 2* mines the iconography of the past and changes it into something quite different, conforming well to his definition. From a distance, the work resembles a map of a cemetery or a guide that a tourist might encounter when visiting a historic site. Without looking closely, one is able to assume that the objects represented are recognizable and typical. However, upon closer examination it becomes apparent that these things are not from the world as we know it.

Under the pristine, computer-generated surface of the print lies a disturbing theme of violence, disease, and decay—a leg grows out of an obelisk; one figure has legs rising up where its torso should be; other sculptures are missing limbs or simply crumbling away. At the center of the "map" a monument lies broken and shattered. Within many of the sculptures, there is a morphing of both different cultures and periods—an Egyptian striding figure is melded with the multiple arms of an Indian Shiva and a classicized goddess holds a machine gun. Some imagery is repeated, including the figure of a child kneeling to pray and a toppled male head, with the specific significance of these symbols remaining open to interpretation. Importantly, in light of Chan's title, within some of the objects buildings and cityscapes seem to take shape. Chan's work, where nothing is as it seems, introduces an alternative reality that raises questions about history, communal memory, and the often unspoken trauma inherent in both.

MWL

Chan, Paul, "Sublime Humility: Notes on Outsider Art and Politics—After 9/11." *National Philistine*. http://www.nationalphilistine.com

Grumiller, Alina Viola. "Hope of Escape: An Interview with Artist Paul Chan." *ARTWURL* (summer 2003). http://www.ps122.org/artwurl.

Kerr, Merrily. "Recuperating Revolt: Aaron Spangler, Paul Chan, and Catherine Sullivan." *Flash Art* (May–June 2004): 106–9.

Saltz, Jerry. "Babylon Rising." *Village Voice* (September 10–16, 2003): 97.

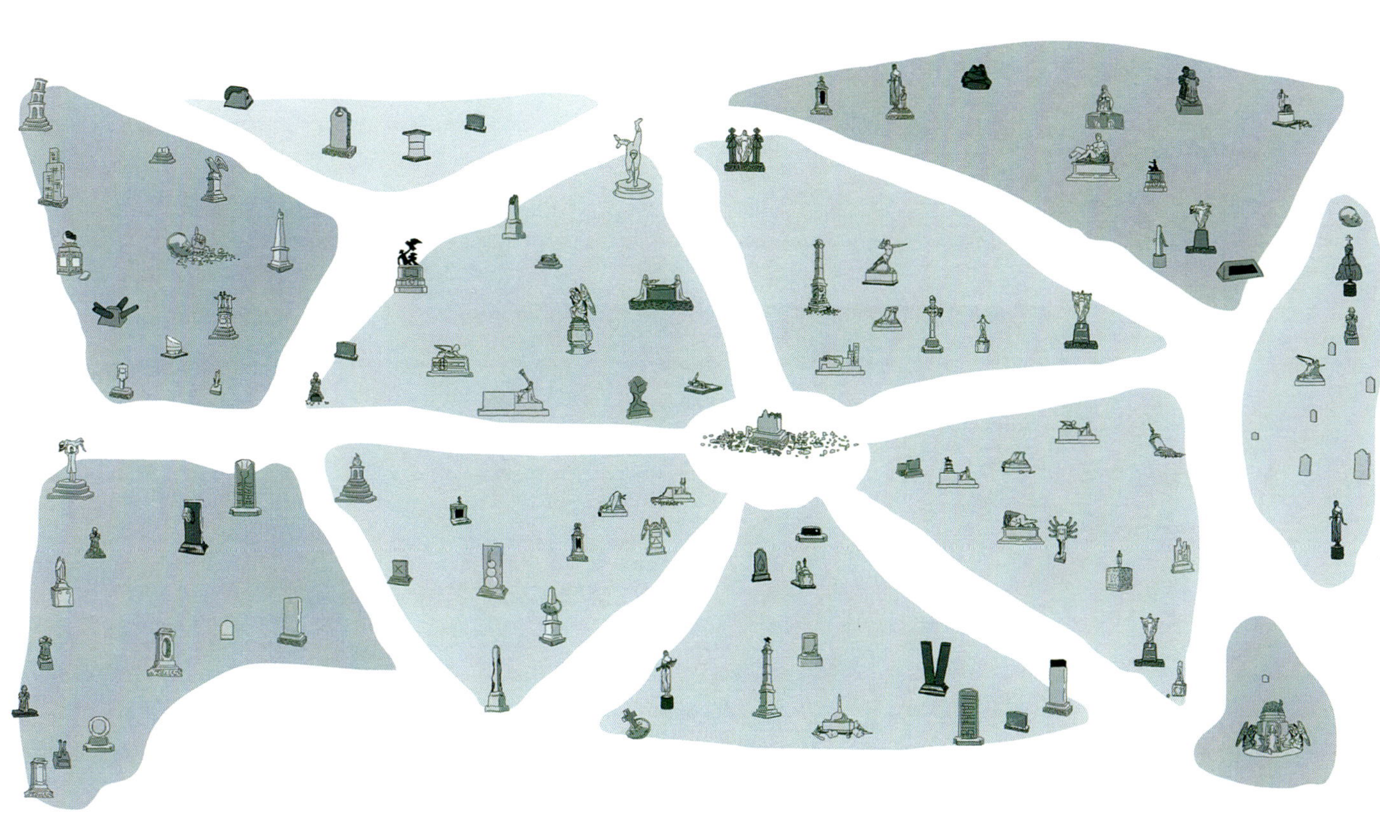

45 **MATTHEW PILLSBURY**

American, born 1973

George Spencer, Seducing the Babysitter, Tuesday, April 1, 2003, 11–12 am

Print 6 of 10
Printed 2005
Pigment ink print
30 x 40 in.

Gift of Maggie Hunt, Class of 1978

Image courtesy of the artist and Bonni Benrubi Gallery, New York

An American born and raised in France, Matthew Pillsbury graduated from Yale University in 1995, where he received the Ethel Child Walker Prize for outstanding undergraduate artist; he completed his M.F.A. at the New York School of Visual Arts in 2004. He was recently chosen as a runner-up in the *New York Times Magazine*'s "Capture the Times" photography contest for his series *Screen-Lives*, which explores the problem of integrating technology into daily life. While the internet and television have made the world a smaller place, they have also succeeded in physically isolating people from one another. In this series, Pillsbury takes black-and-white, long-exposure photographs of family and friends sitting alone in their apartments. The long-exposure photographs reduce the images of people to mere ghosts, and the strong light emitted from the television and computer screens highlights the details of the rooms in which the people sit alone and isolated. The portraits are therefore created from the objects and possessions in the room, while the sitters literally vanish into thin air. Pillsbury explains that the thrill of these portraits lies in the very absence of figures: "With the room's inhabitants somewhat absent, the photographs edge toward the voyeuristic," he says. "The viewer enters private spaces and can linger over the smallest details" (Jacobs 2004).

George Spencer, Seducing the Babysitter, Tuesday April 1, 2003, 11–12 am comes from *Screen-Lives*. Pillsbury was inspired by Hiroshi Sugimoto's long-exposure shots of movie theater interiors that are illuminated by movie screens alone. He desired to apply the same formal technique in more intimate or off-putting settings: his friends' bedrooms, living rooms, offices, and studios (Aletti 2004). In *Screen-Lives* Pillsbury uses the length of his subject's favorite TV show or internet browsing to dictate his exposure time. "Television and computer screens have fundamentally altered the rhythm and content of our lives, and we have not questioned the change," Pillsbury has stated. "I'm interested in how we incorporate them into our lives and interact with them" (Brown 2004). This photograph emphasizes the ephemeral nature of the human body, compared with the permanence of the objects in the surrounding room. Pillsbury questions the ease with which technology has taken over people's lives by showing the TV as the only source of light in the picture.

VVC

Aletti, Vince. "Show World: Matthew Pillsbury at Bonni Benrubi Gallery." *Village Voice* (5 July 2004).

Brown, Janelle. "Time Warp." *Wired Magazine*. Iss. 12.05 (May 2004).

Jacobs, Kate. "The Runners-Up." *New York Times Magazine* (13 June 2004).

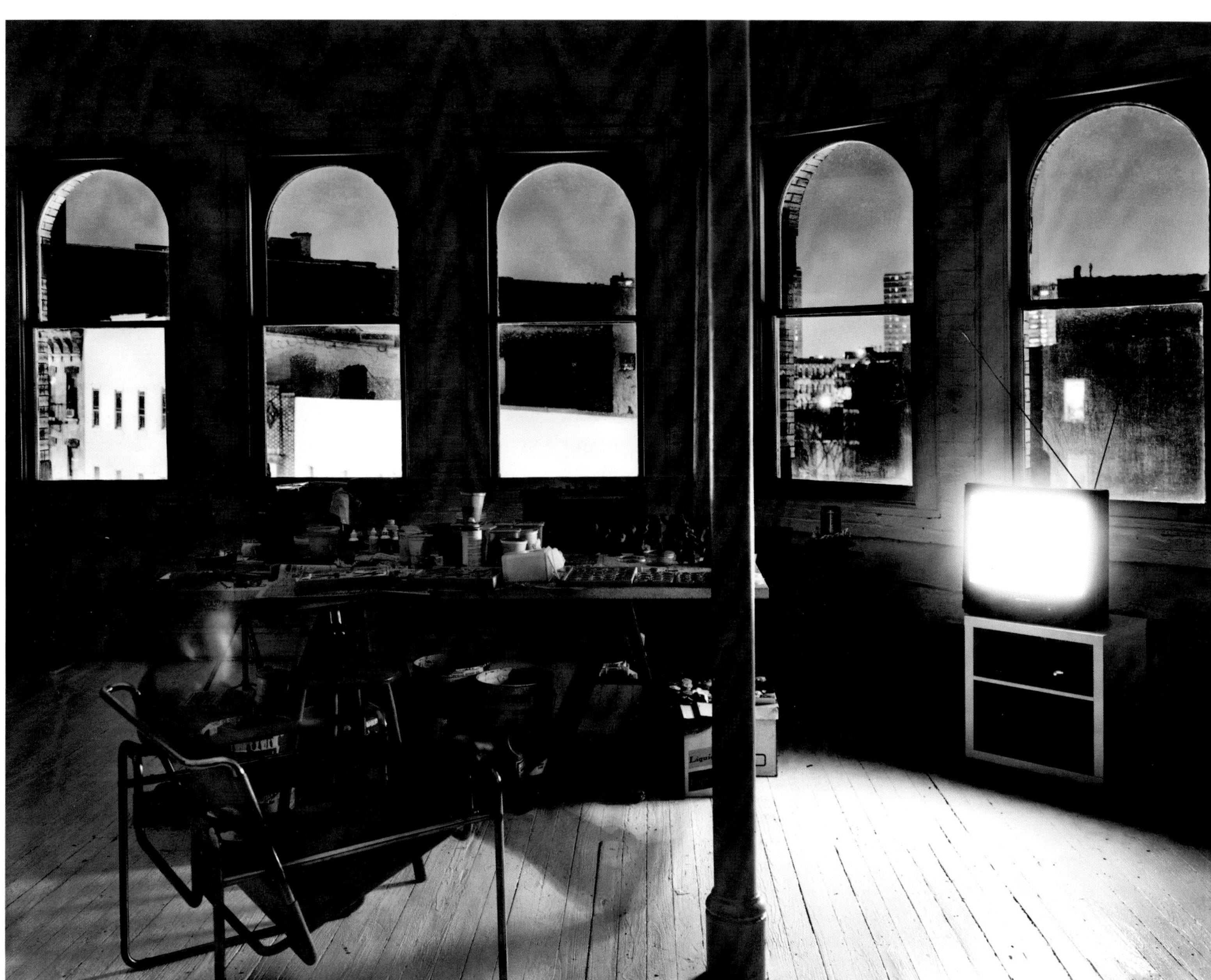

Named Spaces of the Hood Museum of Art

The Dorothy M. Shapiro Pavilion
The Ivan Albright Gallery
The Gene Y. Kim Gallery
The Alvin P. Gutman Gallery
The Israel Sack Gallery
The Bedford Courtyard
The Fowler Gateway
The Sanders Seminar Room
The Barrows Print Room
The Arthur M. Loew Auditorium
The Harrington Gallery
The William B. Jaffe and Evelyn A. Jaffe Hall Galleries
The Dorothy and Churchill Lathrop Gallery
The Friends Gallery
The Owen Robertson Cheatham Gallery
The Bernstein Study-Storage Center

Acquisitions Endowments

The Adelbert Ames Jr. 1919 Fund
The Anonymous #144 Fund
The Katharine T. and Merrill G. Beede 1929 Fund
The Class of 1935 Memorial Fund
The Contemporary Art Fund
The Fund for Contemporary Photography
The Harry Shafer Fisher 1966 Memorial Fund
The Kira Fournier/Benjamin Schore Sculpture Fund
The Phyllis and Bertram Geller 1937 Memorial Fund
The Sondra and Charles Gilman Jr. Foundation Fund
The Alvin and Mary Bert Gutman '40 Acquisition Fund
The Mrs. Harvey P. Hood W'18 Fund
The Hood Museum of Art Acquisitions Fund
The William B. Jaffe and Evelyn A. Jaffe Hall Fund
The William B. and Evelyn A. Jaffe ('58,'60, '63) Fund
The Virginia and Preston T. Kelsey '58 Fund
The John M. MacDonald 1940 Fund
The Guernsey Center Moore 1904 Memorial Fund
The Florence and Lansing Porter Moore 1937 Fund
The Claire and Richard P. Morse 1953 Fund
The Olivia H. and John O. Parker '58 Acquisition Fund
The William S. Rubin Fund
The Stephen and Constance Spahn '63 Acquisition Fund
The Miriam and Sidney Stoneman Acquisition Fund
The Robert J. Strasenburg II 1942 Fund
The Charles F. Venrick 1936 Fund
The Jean and Adolph Weil Jr. 1935 Fund
The Julia L. Whittier Fund
The Charles J. and Opel Zimmerman 1923 Fund

Donors of Art and Artifacts and Funds toward Acquisitions, Hood Museum of Art, 1985–2005

The following lists focus on donors who have made a contribution to the Hood Museum of Art's permanent collection, either through the donation of works of art and artifacts or funds toward the direct purchase of works of art. The funds raised through the members of the Lathrop Fellows of the Hood Museum of Art are also devoted to the purchase of art for the museum's collections.

Donors of Art and Artifacts, 1985–March 2005

Anna Achenbach
Josephine Patterson Albright GP'83
Estate of Ivan Albright
Alexander Reeves Fine Art
American Academy and Institute of Arts and Letters, New York
Helen and Paul Anbinder
Roger Arvid Anderson '68
Marjorie Van Antwerp W'21
Anonymous Donors
Estate of Colonel John L. Ames Jr. '16
Lawrence A. Armour '56, Tu'57
Ethel and Robert E. Asher '31, GP'88
Mr. and Mrs. Gilbert L. Augenblick '43, Tu'44, P'79
Jacquelynn Baas
Anne Bacon
Gladys and Everett Bacon
Mr. and Mrs. H. W. Bacon P'71
Charles Balch
Bequest of Eileen P. Barber
Eileen K. Barfuss '84

Mr. and Mrs. J. J. Barr
Guillermo Alberto Prieto Barral
Lisa and Leonard Baskin
Catherine M. Bearce '85
Rosemarie Beck
Rosemarie Beck Foundation
Katharine T. and Merrill G. Beede '29
L. Graeme Bell III '66
Bruce Bennett
Mirte Berko GP'02
James A. Bergquist
Jane and Raphael Bernstein P'87,'89
Ann and Joel Berson '49
Mr. and Mrs. Jake Berthot
Mr. and Mrs. Eugene L. Berenbach
David Bindman
August Robert Birmelin
Ilse Bischoff
Estate of Robert S. Black '32
Barbara and James A. Block '59, P'85
Anthony and Lois Blumka
Estate of Ruth Blumka
Marilyn and Varujan Boghosian
James Bohary
Eleanor Bontecou
Arthur E. Bosworth M.D.
John W. Brainerd
Damon Brandt
Richard Brisson
Lois and H. W. Broido Jr. '51, Tu'52
H. Allen Brooks '49
Aldis Browne
Katheryn Corbin and Jeffrey R. Brown '61
Michael S. Brown '70
Peter T. Brown '63, P'91
Marilyn Brunson

Mr. and Mrs. Michael Burley
Dan Bush
Judith Byfield
Catherine H. Campbell
Helaine and Paul S. Cantor '60, P'93
Frieda and Prentiss Carnell '56, TH'57, Tu'57
Ninon and Bernard Chaet
Mrs. Waldo Chamberlain
Charles M. Young Fine Prints and Drawings LLC
Robert Chenard
Robert W. Christy
William S. Clark '42, Tu'47, P'75
Jane Clarkin
Helen Cleveland '80
Mrs. Clark Clifford
Patricia W. Clement
Richard E. and Carole P. Cocks
Sharon Cohen
Ellen and Theodore Conant
Elizabeth E. Craig
William P. Curry '57
Jane and W. David Dance '40, Tu'41, P'77, GP'99
Robert Dance '77
Ara Danikian
Dartmouth Class of 1958
Dartmouth Class of 1961
Dartmouth Class of 1962
Martha R. Daura
Franklin Davidson, M.D. '55
Thomas G. Davies '62
Joseph Davis III '36
Denenberg Fine Arts, San Francisco
Monroe A. Denton Jr. '68
Joan M. and Robert M. Desky P'87
Mr. and Mrs. S. Whitney Dickey P'89
Ellen F. and Anthony H. Dingman '57
Mrs. Lucia Dunlop Dillon
Andrew Donaldson Jr. '34

William T. Doran Jr. '30
Bequest of Michael A. Dorris
Estates of Gladys and Franklin Ford Doten '23
Gregory Drake '83
Harriet S. Drew
Betty M. and Douglas M. Duffy '42
Elizabeth and Lane Dwinell '28, Tu'29, H'55
Dr. Donald S. Dworken '51
Marc Efron '65 and Barbara Bares
Estate of Samuel Eilenberg
Burton Elliott '48, Th'48, P'76, P'86
Mary Regensburg Feist
Teddy and Stanley Feldberg '46, P'73,'74
Natalie E. and John E. Fenn M.D. '54, P'84
Suzanne B. and Waldo L. Fielding M.D. '43, DMS'43
Charles H. Flanders
Andrew Forge
Reginald Foster III P'86
Bequest of Frederick D. Forsch '37
Jon Gilbert Fox and Darrell Hotchkiss '71
Harry A. Franklin Family
Valerie Franklin
Mrs. John French
Hugh J. Freund '67, P'08
Dr. Abraham M. Friedman
Dr. Kenneth Friedman
Mr. and Mrs. Clifford J. Fuller Jr. '42
Michael Gallis
Jane Garrison
Elizabeth and Mark Gates Jr. '59, P'83,'91
Gaultney-Klineman Art, Inc.

Alan B. Gazzaniga M.D. '58, DMS'59, P'89
Ilse Getz
LaVerne and Thomas George '40
Richard J. Giarrusso '66
Peter Michael Gish '49, P'84
Charles Giuliano
Ira Glackens
David R. Godine '66
Robert A. and Dorothy H. Goldberg
Hilliard T. Goldfarb
Louis M. Goldich
Carl Golub P'83
Carol and James Goodfriend
Nancy D. and Lane W. Goss '55, P'84,'89
Malcolm and Catherine Greenough
Greenwich Workshop
Neil Grossman '65, P'86,'92,'94
Estate of Musa Guston
Kenneth and Sara Hale
Michael Hall
Joel M. Halpern
Finny Ham
Jamie and Haim Handwerker
Hanover Historical Society
Mrs. W. A. Hanna
Professor Elmer Harp Jr.
Diantha C. and George C. Harrington '61
Louise C. (Mrs. Frank L.) Harrington W'24, P'61
Bequest of Virginia P. and Creighton C. Hart '28, P'56,'58, GP'80,'85
Margot Grace Hartmann and Frank Hartmann '43
Nanatte and Allan Harvey
Emily Harvey and Christian Xatrec
George Herman '41, P'80,'83
Allerton C. Hickmott '17
Orton H. Hicks Jr. '49, Tu'50
Josiah F. Hill '56

Polly B. and Richard D. Hill '41, Tu'42, H'73, P'74,'76, GP'05
Frederic F. and Doris Marston Hillier
Elisabeth and Arthur R. Hills '41, Tu'42, P'67,'68,'72
Eileen and Crawford Hinman '37, P'70,'75,'80
Jeffrey Hinman '68
Margaret J. and Arthur D. Hittner '71
Ethel C. and Herbert E. Hirschland '39
Paul W. Hodes '72
Robert B. Hodes '46, Tu'47, P'72
Margaret and John L. Hoffman
Frank H. Hogan
Irene Hollister
Charles H. Hood II '51
Russell and John Huber '63
Jim Hunt and Maggie Fellner Hunt '78
Alice Hutchins
Estate of Lydia G. Hutchinson W'20
Dr. A. Everett James Jr.
Joan and Victor Johnson
Bequest of Mrs. Berkeley Fairfax Jones W'25
Emily Henderson Graves Jones
Mary Katherine Burton Jones
Lynn and John Kearney
Mary Alice and William R. Keast
Richard J. Kempe
Mel Kendrick
Melitta Kern-Hammond
Mary Neidlinger Kilmarx and Peter H. Kilmarx '83
Robert Dudley Kilmarx '50, Tu'51, H'72, P'83
Wan and Andrew B. Kim P'85
B. A. King
Elizabeth J. and Victor R. King '31, P'59, GP'95
Remsen M. Kinne III '52
Hedy and Kent M. Klineman '54, P'89,'92
Kent M. Klineman '54, P'89,'92
Joseph Knopfelmacher
Dr. Stanley Kogan '52
Shelley Kolton
Sarah-Ann and Werner H. Kramarsky P'92
Edward Lamb '24, H'82
Susan Landgraf
Connie and Frederick Landmann
Mark Lansburgh '49, P'77,'88
Family of Mark Lansburgh '49, '77, '88
Catherine C. Lastavica M.D.
Mr. and Mrs. Edward Connery Lathem '51
Vera Lateiner
John K. Lee '78
Paula and Mack Lee
Pamela G. and Arnold L. Lehman P'95
M. Rosalie Leidinger and Louise W. Schmidt
Barbara and I. Robert Levine '54, Tu'55, P'80,'82
Elaine and Gerald D. Levine Tu'63
Robert A. Levinson '46, Tu'46
Harry T. Lewis Jr. '55, Tu'56, P'81
Mr. and Mrs. Herbert Libertson
Madeleine and Stephen Lister '63
William E. Little '31
Louis and Shirley LoMonaco
Mrs. Bryan J. Lynch
Frances S. MacIntyre MALS'90
Susan Stedman Majors
Susan R. Malloy P'83
Dr. Samuel Mandel
Stephen F. Mandel '52, P'78,'81
Carla and John M. Manley '40, Tu'41
Blanche and Leo Manso
Edward B. Marks '32, P'65
Tancie and Dave Martin '29, P'54
Charlotte Mathey
Brantz and Ana Mayor
Elizabeth R. Mayor
Michael Mazur
Patricia McHugh
Estates of Catherine L. and Robert A. McKennan '25
Claire and Dr. Frederick R. Mebel '35
Micaela and Jack Mendelsohn '56
Christopher Mendez
John L. Miller
Leonore O. Miller
Richard H. Miller
Hilary B. Miller '73, Tu'74
Lucia Fairchild Taylor Miller
Nancy and John Milne M.D. '37, DMS'38, P'67,'70
Bequest of William J. Mitchel Jr. '42
Mary K. Modeen-Watkinson
Frank W. Molloy '68
Montshire Museum of Science
Charles Willard Moore
Jean and Ben Frank Moss
John H. Mudie '49
Polly W. and Richard Muzzy '35, Tu'36
Ned P. Nabers '60
Jenifer Neils
Sylvia (Mrs. Harry D.) Nelson Tu'52
Steve Newman
Douglas Newton
Bruce H. Nichols
Jane and Victor A. Noel Jr.
John S. North '52, Tu'53, P'85
Joe Novak '52, Tu'53
Carl Frederick Oman '86
Jane Oman W'56, P'86
Bart Osman '90, Tu'96
Harley and Stephen Osman '56, Tu'57, P'80,'90,Tu'96
Scott Osman '80
Jeanne S. Overstreet
Ann Parker
Olivia H. and John O. Parker '58, Tu'59, P'89,'91,Tu'94
Francis Parkman Jr.
Henry Parkman
Samuel Parkman
Theodore B. Parkman
Chris P. Paterson
Carol Patten
Paul W. Worman Fine Art
J. Robert Peacock '68
Morton Pechter '43, Tu'44, P'73,'75, GP'04
Francis R. Peisch '39, P'70,'75,'82
Mark L. Peisch '44
Gabor F. Peterdi
Marta (Mrs. David F.) Phillips W'51
Alice Pollard
Bequest of E. Grosvenor Plowman '20
Bernard H. and Suzanne Pucker
Keith Quinton '80
Elizabeth and Guido R. Rahr Sr. P'51
Russell D. Reddig
Audrey S. and J. Dudley Richards '39
Eric Richards
Louise Riegel
John Norman Rines

Leandro P. Rizzuto
Estate of Mary C. Rockefeller P'54, GP'79,'86,Tu'92
Rodman C. Rockefeller '54
Ellis L. Rolett
Stewart G. Rosenblum '70
Barbara and Jay Rosenfield '49, P'77,'88
Dr. and Mrs. Walter S. Rothwell '45, DMS'45
Jay E. Rothmeier '79
Deiter and Si Rosenkranz
Alice M. Runyon
Julia and Richard H. Rush '37, Tu'38
Dr. and Mrs. Stuart Russell
Sarajean and David C. Ruttenberg
Ira Sachs
Schmeckebier Family
Robert and Mary Schmid
Louise W. Schmidt
Charles B. Schudson '72, P'02
Sarah and George W. Schoenhut
Professor Emeritus and Mrs. Harry Schultz '37
M. R. Schweitzer
John and Mallory Semple
George T. M. Shackelford '77
Molly Grover Shallow
Dr. Daniel C. Shannon
Antoinette M. and Edward Shapiro '62
Joel Shapiro
Fazal Sheikh
Mrs. Merle Shera
Sonia Landy Sheridan
Mrs. Les Sholty
Daniel E. Siedler '77
Gilbert B. Silverman
Ruth (Mrs. Norman) Simon W'36, P'64
Susan S. and William A. Small Jr.
Smoyer Family, in memory of William Smoyer '67
Joan P. Snell '73
Barbara Eck Sorini
Blake Spahn
Contance and Stephen H. Spahn '63, P'99
Kirk Spahn '99
Margaret E. Spicer
Charles Spurrier
Dr. and Mrs. David G. Stahl '47
Children of Justin A. Stanley '33, P'71, H'83, GP'01
Professor James L. Steffensen Jr.
Family of Joseph Stein '38
Caroline and Ralph Steiner '21, H'86
Joel Sternfeld '65
Frank P. Stetz
Margaret S. (Mrs. Robert Nichols) Stevens W'27
Mary Louise Warden (Mrs. Kenneth A.) Stewart Tu'75W
Eugene P. Stichman '57, P'94
Richard E. Stoiber '32, P'71
Alan N. Stone and D. Lesley Hill
Mrs. Douglas Storer W'21
Lou Stoumen
Arnold and Joanne Syrop
Bernice and Joseph Tanenbaum
Dr. Radford C. Tanzer '25
Kathleen A. Tefft
Jan and Chan Tenney
David J. Teplica DMS'85
Carola B. Terwilliger
Virginia V. Thorndike
Hugh and Mary Townley
Lois B. Torf and Adrienne B. Torf
Cynthia N. Travers
Dorothy G. and Herman J. Trefethen '26, P'63
Steven Trefonides
Ruth Tulving
Bequest of Ellen T. Turner
David Usher '62
Nancy and Heinz Valtin
Jan van der Marck
Charles and Gloria Vogel
Mary and Peter A. Vogt '47, P'79
Peter H. Voulkos
Hugh Mason Wade
Audrey Webster
Jean and Adolph Weil Jr. '35
Catherine Dail Weil '85
Howard L. Weinberg '62
Benjamin Weiss
Barbara Wellington Wells
Mrs. J. Mattocks White
Frederick B. Whittemore '53, Tu'54, P'88,'90, H'03
Jean L. Whitnack
Mr. and Mrs. John R. Williams Jr. '56
Virginia (Mrs. Gordon) Williamson W'62
Stephen W. Winship '41
Philip Wofford
Helen Wolff H'86
Heidi and Arthur Lewis Wood Ph.D. '34
Charles T. Wood P'81,'82
Mrs. Edward J. Wynkoop
Christina Yang
David and Constance Yates
Tessim Zorach
Timothy Zorach

Donors of Funds for the Purchase of Works of Art, 1985–2005

William R. Acquavella
Jane and Henry Adams
Chauncey N. Allen '24
Francis and George Armour Foundation
Earl Arthurs '35
Dongkyu Bak '57, P'83
George F. Baker Trust
Richard H. Barr '55
Diana and Richard Beattie '61, P'89
Kirsten and Peter Bedford P'89
G. Dandelot Belin
Phoebe Bender
Karen Berlin '89
Marguerite and Lee P. Berlin
Raphael Bernstein P'87,'89
Bernstein Development Foundation
Lucretia A'51 and Peter Martin '51, P'83
Karen and Alfred A. Blum Jr.
Johnson S. Bogart
Jules Bromberg '35, DMS'36
Bruce L. Brown '41
Dorothy and Benjamin Burch '32
Amelie and B. Bernei Burgunder Jr. '41, Tu'42, P'77
Constance and Walter Burke '44, GP'90, H'94
Frances L. Burnett
Eleanor Caldwell
Gayle and Andrew Camden
Barbara E. Carpenter
Lauren and Derrick Cartwright
Robert W. Christy
William S. Clark '42, Tu'47, P'75
Carolyn Kohn '76
Lewis D. Cole '35

Virginia and John Cornehlsen '29, P'64
Elizabeth E. Craig
Carlyle W. Crane '35
The Cremer Foundation
Prudence M. Dame
Jane and W. David Dance '40, Tu'41, P'77, GP'99
Dartmouth Class of 1951
Dartmouth Class of 1952
Dartmouth Class of 1955
Corinne Davidson
H. Allan Dingwall Jr. '42
Carol and Rodney Dubois '57, Tu'58
G. Cameron Duncan '35, P'64
John J. Eagan Jr. '35
Robert D. Eckerson '48
Estate of Josephine Albright GP'83
Estate of Russell Cowles '09, H'51
Estate of David S. Hull '60
Exxon Corporation
Iris and Robert Fanger '55, P'89
Maxwell R. Feinberg '35, Tu'36
Barbara and Oscar H. Feldman
Rita and Kenneth Fischbeck
Richard A. Florsheim
Hugh J. Freund '67, P'08
The Friends of the Hopkins Center and Hood Museum of Art
Charles W. Gaillard '62
Elizabeth and Mark Gates Jr. '59, P'83,'91
Joseph H. Geller P'92
General Electric Corporation
General Mills Corporation
LaVerne and Thomas George '40
John L. Giegerich Jr. '51, Tu'52
Peter M. Gish '49, P'84
Frederick Goldstein
Sondra W'52, P'91 and Celso Gonzales-Falla
Esther Grover
Frederick T. Haley '35, P'74,'77
F. Gordon Hamlin '35, P'65
Harbert, Marietta, Deloitte, Merriam
Louise and Frank L. Harrington '24, P'50,'54,'61
Frank Harrington Jr.'50
Diantha and George Harrington '61
Thomas Harrington '54, Tu'57
Mrs. Walter E. Hart
Mary and John Hatch '51, P'80
Eric Hawke '35
Hermit Hill Charitable Trust
Wallace Hodges '35, Tu'36, P'66,'68, GP'97
Mari-Elizabeth Hoffman
Katherine and Harry Hood
H. P. Hood, Incorporated
Thomas M. Hotaling '73
Frank E. Hotchkiss '50
Howard Scripps Foundation
John L. Huber '63
Martha Ingraham
Susan and Gary Jacobson
John J. Jerve
Rachel and James Jordan
Judy and Earle Kazis
Jane M. and Richard L. Kaufmann
Mr. and Mrs. Richard J. Kelly
A. Amy Kilkenny '84
Carolyn Kohn '76
Sarah and Werner H. Kramarsky P'92
Richard M. Lansburgh '43
Katherine Larmon
Edward Connery Lathem '51
Caroline Lathrop
Ann R. Leven
Patricia and Robert Levinson '46, Tu'46
The R. C. Lilly Foundation
Peter Lihatsh
William E. Little '31
Jane and Richard Lombard '53, Tu'54, P'88
Alan F. Markovitz
Adele Baron Marks W'30
Winslow Martin '44
Seglem/Peat Marwick Foundation
William H. Mathers '35, P'80
Sheila and Frank E. McGinity
McKinsey & Company, Inc.
Joseph A. Meo
Joseph Millimet '36
Wynne W. Miller
Aaron Milrad
Mobil Corporation
Alice Moir P'89
Charles R. Moon Jr. '35
Mrs. Emerson Morse W'18
Elinor Bunin and George Munroe '43, H'93
Leonard M. Nelson
New Hampshire Potters Guild
Fredric O'Brien '35
Molly O'Connor
Karen B. and Paul H. Orsillo
Herbert H. Ostrow '35, Tu'36, P'67, GP'96
A. Brooks Parker '55, Tu'56, P'85,'90
Patricia and Nathan W. Pearson Jr. '32
Robert Perkins '55
David V. Picker '53
Pierrepont Associates
George Price '35, P'67, GP'93
Prospero Foundation
Jan Seidler Ramirez '73
Maurice Rapf '35, P'68
Kenneth I. Reich '60
Diane and Leslie Riman
Katherine Duff '71 and John R. Rines
Samuel R. Roberts
Rodman Rockefeller '54
Kenneth Roman '52
Steven Roth '62, Tu'63, P'93
Timothy F. Rub A'35
Julia and Richard Rush '37, Tu'38
Claude Saucier '75
Donald Saunders '35
Schering-Plough Foundation
Robert J. Scholnick
Mary Anne Schwalbe
Robert Searles '42, P'74, GP'85
Emilia Seibold '82
Jerome Siegel
Stephen Simon Trust
Helen and J. Donald Smiley M.D. P'79,'82
Donald H. Smith '48, Tu'49
Marilyn and Peter J. Smith '48, P'73
Robert S. Smith'67, P'98,'04
Mrs. Walter A. Sobel
Barbara Dau Southwell '78
Roxanna and John Stevenson
Helen E. Stoddard
Leila and Melville Straus '60, P'92
Frances and Gilbert Tanis '38, P'71, GP'93
Richard F. Upton '35
Peter Vogt '47, P'79
John Wallace '35, Tu'36, P'72
Charles Weinberg '42, Th'42, P'74
Arthur S. Wensinger '48
Mary Lou and Harry Wildasin M.D.
Beverly and Daniel H. Wolf
Susan A'69 and James Wright '64
Matthew Wysocki
Xerox Corporation
William I. Zeitung '43

Current Lathrop Fellows of the Hood Museum of Art

Brooke and James Adler '60, Tu'61, P'89
Kirsten and Peter Bedford P'89
Charlotte and Charles Bimba Jr.
Debra and Leon Black '73
Harriet Warm and Richard Blum '53, P'85,'90
Constance and Walter Burke '44, GP'90, H'94
Judy and Russell Carson '65, P'95
Patricia Hewitt and Dale Christensen Jr. '69, P'02
Marilyn and Robert Clements '54, P'83,'86
Allison Morrow and Jonathan L. Cohen '60, Tu'61
Robert Dance '77
Marianne and Thomas Davies '62
Carol and Rodney DuBois '57, Tu'58
Nancy and Donald Dworken M.D. '51
Barbara Bares and Marc Efron '65
Anne and John Feighner M.D. P'06
Theodora Feldberg P'73,'74
Hugh Freund Esq. '67, P'08
Elizabeth and Mark Gates Jr. '59, P'83,'91
W. Patrick Gramm '52, P'88
Mary Bert and Alvin Gutman '40
Nancy Newcomb and John Hargraves '66
Judy and Charles Hood '51
Margaret Fellner '78 and James Hunt
Virginia Rice A'61 and Preston Kelsey II '58, P'82,'88,'90
Joan and Remsen Kinne III '52
Patricia and Robert Levinson '46, Tu'46
Andrew Lewin '81
Charles Liddle III '52, Tu'53, P'83
Madeleine and Stephen Lister '63
Lucretia A'51 and Peter Martin '51, P'83
Sally and William Neukom '64, P'90,'91,'97
Nancy and Thomas O'Neil III '79
Olivia and John O. Parker '58, Tu'59, P'89,'91,'94
Beverly and David Payne '58
Ray Powers Jr. '49
Jan Seidler Ramirez '73
Barbara and James Reibel M.D. '63, P'03
Linda and Frederick Roesch '60, Tu'61, P'88,'90
Shirley and Henry Sanders '51
Benjamin Schore
Barbara Dau '78 and David Southwell Tu'88
Constance and Stephen Spahn '63, P'99
Judith and Richard Steinberg '54, Tu'55, P'86,'88
Leila and Melville Straus '60, P'92
Ann and Richard von Hoorn
Gail Wasson P'96
Virginia and Robert Weil '40, P'73
Gretchen '77 and Robert Wetzel '76
Joanne and Walter Wilson '58, P'84
Joanne and Douglas Wise '59
M. Paul Zimmerman '55, P'81

Former Lathrop Fellows of the Hood Museum of Art

Josephine Albright GP'83
Maxwell Anderson '77
Anne and H. Wood Bacon
Judith Welling and De Witt Baker III '46, Tu'47, P'78
William Banks Jr. '45
R. Susan and Bryce Bastian '54, P'96
Susan and Marvin Baten '56, Tu'57, P'86
Diana and Richard Beattie '61, P'89
Claudia Cooley and L. Graeme Bell III '66
Marcy and Joseph Caldwell III '51, Tu'52, P'85,'89
Barbara Carpenter
Mildred and Lo-Yi Chan '54, P'80,'83,'88, H'04
Marjorie and Russell Cook '53, Tu'57, P'82,'87
Robert M. Cummings '42
Susannah Drake Culhane '87
Margaret Tu'89 and Henry Erbe III '84
Helen and Peter Fahey '68, Th'70, P'92,'94,'97,'06
Marcia and John A. Friede '60, P'83
Howard Gilman '44, Tu'45
Deborah and Sidney Goldman M.D. '60
Jerome Goldstein '54, P'92
Robert Grinnell
Evelyn A. J. Hall P'58,'60,'63, GP'83
Diantha and George Harrington '61
Frederick Henry '67, P'90,'91
William Jones '49
Sarah and Werner Kramarsky P'92
Margaret Clancy and Asher Lans '38
Ann Leven
Jane Lombard W'53, WTu'54, P'88
Mary Ann and Barry MacLean '60, Th'61, P'87,'94,'95, H'91
Skipwith and David Mechlin '72
Florence Moore W'37
Marian and W. Bradley Morehouse '46
Elinor Bunin and George Munroe '43, H'77,'93
Mark Myers '75
John Oberdorfer '66
Jane and Richard Page '54, P'81,'86, H'90,'04
Patricia and Nathan Pearson '32
Marta Phillips W'51
Ellen and Kenneth Roman '52
Janet and Allen W. Root M.D. '55, DMS'56, P'82,'85
Nancy and Stewart Sanders '56
Brinna and Frank Sands II '58, P'87,'95
James Skiles III '66
Helen and J. Donald Smiley M.D. P'79,'82
Miriam and Sidney Stoneman '33, GP'88,'90
Edward Storrs '55
Mary Lou and Peter Vogt '47, P'79
Celeste and Stephen Weisglass
Maud '77 and Jeffrey Welles '77
Karen and Thomas Wise M.D. '65, P'05

Hood Museum of Art Staff

Jourdan Abel, *Registrarial Assistant*
Gary Alafat, *Security/Buildings Manager*
Mike Balog, *Security Guard*
Kristin Bergquist, *School and Family Programs Coordinator*
Juliette Bianco, *Exhibitions Manager*
Theresa Delemarre, *Administrative Assistant for Development*
Amy Driscoll, *Assistant Curator of Education*
Patrick Dunfey, *Exhibitions Designer/Preparations Supervisor*
Cynthia Gilliland, *Assistant Registrar*
Kellen Haak, *Collections Manager/Registrar*
Mary Ann Hankel, *Exhibitions and Events Coordinator*
Katherine Hart, *Interim Director* and *Barbara C. and Harvey P. Hood 1918 Curator of Academic Programming*
Deborah Haynes, *Data Manager*
Linda Ide, *Tour Coordinator*
Alfredo Jurado, *Security Guard*
Margaret Lind, *Assistant Curator*
Barbara MacAdam, *Jonathan L. Cohen Curator of American Art*
Lisa Mackie, *Receptionist*
Nancy McLain, *Business Manager*
Nils Nadeau, *Editor and Publications Coordinator*
Kathleen O'Malley, *Associate Registrar*
Sharon Reed, *Public Relations Coordinator*
John Reynolds, *Lead Preparator*
Mary Ellen Rigby, *Gift Shop Manager*
Roberta Shin, *Interim Executive Assistant*
Barbara Thompson, *Curator of African, Oceanic, and Native American Collections*
T. Barton Thurber, *Curator of European Art*
Lesley Wellman, *Curator of Education*
Kathryn Whittaker, *Security Guard*
Janet Whyte, *Security Guard*
Matthew Zayatz, *Preparator*

Overseers of Hopkins Center and Hood Museum of Art

Donna Bascom '73
George Berry '66, P'98
Paul Cantor '60, P'93
Judith Carson P'95
Jonathan L. Cohen '60, Tu'61
David F. Frankel M.D. '62
Hugh Freund '67, P'08
Allan H. Glick '60, Tu'61, P'88
Andrew Greenebaum '84, Tu'89
Edward Hansen P'85,'88
Charles Hood '51
Margaret Fellner Hunt '78
Pamela J. Joyner '79
Robert Levinson '46, Tu'46
David Mechlin '72
Jan Seidler Ramirez '73
James Reibel M.D. '63, P'03
Bonnie Reiss P'06
Thomas Ruegger '76, P'06
Benjamin Schore
David Slade '76, P'03
Barbara Dau Southwell '78
Norman Steinberg P'02
Deborah Hope Wedgeworth '76, P'01
Robert Weil '40, P'73
Robert O. Wetzel '76

Friends of Hopkins Center and Hood Museum of Art Board of Directors, 2004–5

Charlotte Bimba
Nancy Cole
Marguerite Collier
Martha Davis
David Milne
Henry Nachman
Sylvia Nelson
Marcus Ratliff
Fran Sherley
Lynne Stahler
Gordon Thomas
Susan Valence
Lynne Whitacre
Steven Whitman